I0171614

Copyright

Published by:
Humbolton Press

www.Humbolton.com

Dallas, Texas

First Edition: 2025

ISBN: 978-1-966703-00-6

About the Author

Ken Konet is a lifelong learner, educator, and corporate learning & development professional with a deep passion for helping others overcome challenges and reach their potential. With a master's in education and two MBAs, Ken has spent decades exploring the intersection of personal development, practical strategies, and science-backed solutions. His career spans IT, Human Resources, Engineering, Business Management and Instructional Design, where he has guided thousands of individuals worldwide through training and enablement programs.

But Ken isn't just someone who teaches these ideas, he is living them! Like many, Ken has faced the struggles of procrastination, endless distractions, and the feeling of being stuck. Balancing a busy professional life with personal growth, he's wrestled with doomscrolling spirals, chaotic schedules, and the inertia loop. These challenges inspired him to dive deep into understanding why we get stuck and, more importantly, how we can move forward. Over the years, Ken has not only studied these concepts but also tested them in his own life, refining practical, actionable steps to build momentum and take control.

Ken roots his approach in real-world experience and infuses it with humor, honesty, and hope, ranging from small, incremental changes to creating meaningful routines. Through his work, Ken has inspired countless individuals to embrace progress over perfection, helping them simplify their lives, conquer distractions, and take actionable steps toward their goals.

With this book, Ken shares the lessons he's learned along the way— lessons that have transformed his life and can do the same for you. When he's not writing or teaching, Ken enjoys exploring the outdoors with his wife Izzy, riding motorcycles, and discovering new ways to balance work, life, and personal growth. His philosophy is simple: life is too short to stay stuck. It's time to embrace the chaos, find your rhythm, and move forward.

Introduction

Welcome to Your New Beginning! Have you ever found yourself lost in an endless scroll, clutching a half-eaten snack, wondering where the day went? You're not alone. In a world designed to distract us, it's easy to lose track of what really matters.

This book isn't here to shame you into changing your life. It's here to help you outsmart the chaos, break free from the inertia loop, and reclaim your time and energy. We'll dive into the science behind why we feel stuck, explore the sneaky traps of modern living—like doomscrolling and junk food binges—and, more importantly, we'll uncover practical, bite-sized solutions to take back control.

With humor, real talk, and actionable advice, you'll learn to trade motivation (which is as fleeting as a TikTok trend) for momentum — a force you can build, sustain, and grow. This isn't just another self-help book. It's a toolkit for breaking free and living a life that feels less like a grind and more like an adventure. Ready to take the first step? Let's do this—together.

Chapter 1: The Doomscrolling Dilemma

The Allure of the Infinite Feed

The allure of the infinite feed can be likened to a buffet where the food is never-ending, but instead of delectable treats, it's a smorgasbord of cat videos, conspiracy theories, and that one friend's vacation photos that make you question your life choices. You start scrolling for just a few minutes, and suddenly it's three hours later, and you've learned way too much about the life cycle of a potato. You might think you're just having a casual evening, but in reality, you've entered a black hole of content that's both mesmerizing and mildly terrifying. Before you know it, you're in a spiral of doomscrolling, where every swipe leads you further down the rabbit hole of chaos, anxiety, and an inexplicable craving for junk food.

Algorithms are the crafty little gremlins behind this digital madness. They know you better than you know yourself, serving up a feast of information tailored to your most bizarre interests. It's like having a personal shopper who has a penchant for the weird and wonderful. One moment you're watching a video about how to bake a cake, and the next, you're knee-deep in conspiracy theories about how cake is actually a government plot. It's funny until it's not, and suddenly you're questioning if your afternoon snack is a harmless treat or a symbol of society's impending doom. The algorithms thrive on your clicks and likes, making it harder to break free from their sticky grip, turning you into an unwitting participant in an echo chamber where negativity reigns supreme.

Now, let's not forget the physical toll this all takes on our bodies. You might think scrolling through memes doesn't count as exercise, but your brain is working overtime! Unfortunately, your body is just sitting there, marinating in a pool of poor nutrition choices and sleep deprivation. The standard American diet of processed foods and sugar highs might feel like a party in your mouth, but your body is throwing a tantrum in the background. It's high time we ditch the junk food for some wholesome snacks that don't leave you feeling like a deflated balloon. Think of it as a personal revolution against the tyranny of empty calories.

Creating a healthy daily routine can feel like trying to solve a Rubik's Cube blindfolded, especially when your space is cluttered with the remnants of your last "I'll clean tomorrow" binge. But here's the kicker: minimalism doesn't mean living in a box with just one spoon and a yoga mat. It means finding clarity in your chaos. By decluttering your physical space, you'll declutter your mind. A tidy space can transform your life from a messy sitcom to a well-scripted drama where you are the star, tackling goals and embracing productivity like a pro. Plus, there's nothing quite like the satisfaction of tossing out old junk that has been taking up space in both your home and your brain.

Ultimately, stepping away from the infinite feed and embracing a mindful approach to technology can make all the difference. It's about finding balance, cultivating positive habits, and learning to prioritize what truly matters. So, go ahead and scroll, but do it with intention! Set timers, take breaks, and make a pact with yourself to swap one binge-scroll session for a walk outside or a good book. You'll find that life beyond the screen is not only fulfilling but also filled with laughter, real connections, and maybe even a few less conspiracy theories. The infinite feed will always be there, but so will the world waiting for you to step out and move forward.

Breaking Up with Your Screen

Breaking up with your screen might feel a bit like trying to end a relationship with that one friend who just won't take the hint. You know, the one who shows up uninvited, always has the latest gossip, and somehow makes you feel both entertained and exhausted at the same time. But let's face it, the time has come to swipe left on the doomscrolling that keeps you glued to your phone like a moth to a flame. You're not just consuming content; you're marinating in it, and it's time to escape that digital marinade before you turn into a full-fledged couch potato. You can trade in those endless hours of scrolling for something a bit more constructive, like, oh I don't know, living your life!

Let's talk about algorithms, those sneaky little devils that know you better than your own mother. They're like that one friend who only brings you to parties where you know everyone just to keep you in your comfort zone. But here's the kicker: they're not doing you any favors. Instead of broadening your horizons, they're trapping you in echo chambers that make you feel like you're the only one who believes pineapple belongs on pizza (which, for the record, it totally does). So, it's time to break free. Start following accounts that challenge your views, engage with content that makes you think, and embrace the chaos of differing opinions. Your brain will thank you, and you might just find some new interests along the way.

Now, let's address the elephant in the room: junk food. You know, that delightful concoction of chemicals and empty calories that seems to scream your name at 2 a.m. It's easy to grab a bag of chips while binging your latest show, but your body isn't a dumpster; it's a temple. And temples need good food, not just whatever is on sale at the gas station. Start prepping healthy snacks and meals that are as colorful as your Instagram feed. Trust me, your body will stop feeling like a deflated balloon, and you'll have more energy to do things other than scrolling through videos of cats doing backflips.

If you find yourself feeling overwhelmed by clutter—be it physical, digital, or emotional—this is your sign to declutter your life. You don't need that pile of old magazines or your fifth pair of shoes that you "might wear someday" (spoiler alert: you won't). Embrace minimalism. It's not just for hipsters; it's a lifestyle that can clear your mind and help you focus on what truly matters. Imagine walking into a clean space where your thoughts aren't competing with the chaos around you. It's like taking a deep breath after being underwater. You'll find it easier to achieve your goals when your environment isn't dragging you down like an anchor.

Finally, let's tackle the elusive concept of a daily routine. You might think routines are boring, but they're like the secret sauce in your favorite dish. They can help you build healthy habits, manage your time, and even improve your sleep. Start small—maybe wake up ten minutes earlier or set a specific time for a quick workout. As you build these habits, you'll notice that inertia starts to lose its grip on you. You'll go from feeling lost and chaotic to being a productivity ninja, slicing through your to-do list like it's made of butter. So, put down that phone, step away from the screen, and take the first step toward a fulfilling life. You've got this!

Finding Joy Beyond the Algorithm

Finding joy beyond the algorithm is like trying to find a unicorn at a tech convention. In a world overwhelmed by digital noise, scrolling endlessly through curated feeds can feel like an Olympic sport, but let's face it—most of us aren't even medaling in that competition. Instead of achieving enlightenment, we often end up knee-deep in an echo chamber of negativity, where the only thing we're truly "liking" is our own despair. So, how do we break free from the clutches of the algorithm and rediscover joy in the real world? Spoiler alert: it involves a tiny bit of effort and a whole lot of laughter.

First, let's tackle the doomscrolling. It's like binge-watching a really bad reality show—at first, you're hooked, but after the third episode, you're just left questioning your life choices. Instead of mindlessly scrolling, try setting a timer for your social media use. When the alarm goes off, treat yourself to something that doesn't require a screen, like a walk outside or a good ol' fashioned book. Yes, those dusty things you may have seen sitting on your shelf. Who knows, you might even find joy in a plot twist that doesn't involve a celebrity meltdown!

Now, let's chat about nutrition, because nothing screams joy like a good serving of kale. Just kidding! But seriously, the standard American diet has turned many of us into junk-food-fueled zombies. Instead of relying on quick fixes like potato chips and soda, why not channel your inner chef? Cooking can be a creative outlet, and it's way more satisfying than waiting for your delivery driver to arrive. Plus, there's nothing quite like the high of making a meal that doesn't come with a side of regret. Picture this: you, a spatula, and an avocado. Pure bliss!

As for clutter, it's like having a never-ending game of hide and seek with your belongings. The more you accumulate, the less you can find anything, including your joy. Embrace minimalism! Start small—maybe tackle that junk drawer that has become a black hole for all things random. You'll be amazed at how liberating it feels to finally locate your favorite pen and a rubber band that's not stuck to a half-eaten granola bar. Decluttering isn't just about tidying up; it's like giving yourself a mental reboot. Joy is waiting just behind that pile of old magazines.

Finally, let's address the elephant in the room: being overwhelmed. Life can feel like a never-ending to-do list, and the pressure to accomplish everything at once can send anyone into a tailspin. Here's a thought—what if you approached your goals like a buffet? Take one thing at a time, savor it, and then move on to the next dish. Instead of trying to eat the whole buffet in one go, relish the process. Remember, joy is often found in the journey, not just the destination, and with a little humor and a lot of heart, you'll find that life beyond the algorithm is not just possible, but downright delightful.

Chapter 2: Echo Chambers and the Sound of One Voice

The Comfort of Like-Mindedness

Imagine this: you stumble into a coffee shop, your phone buzzing with notifications, and the aroma of burnt coffee filling your nostrils. You look around and see a sea of people glued to their screens, likely scrolling through the latest memes about their existential crises. Welcome to the club of like-mindedness, where everyone is either doomscrolling or conspiring against their own productivity. This is the modern support group we never asked for, but here we are, united in our struggle to find meaning in a world of endless TikTok dances and cat videos. The comfort of knowing that others are equally lost in their digital rabbit holes can be oddly reassuring, even if it's all a bit absurd.

Now, let's get real for a second. You might be sitting there, munching on a bag of chips that somehow turned into your new best friend, wondering why you can't muster the energy to transform your life. Spoiler alert: it's not just you. We've all fallen victim to the siren song of the standard American diet, where junk food reigns supreme and vegetables are merely a garnish on our plates. In our quest for comfort, we have unknowingly created a community of junk food aficionados, each one of us just trying to find solace in our low-nutrient choices while sharing memes about kale being the enemy. The truth is, we're all in this together, and it's time we start swapping out those potato chips for something green—if only to give our bodies a fighting chance.

Speaking of fighting chances, let's chat about the inertia loop. You know, that delightful cycle where you plan to accomplish great things, but somehow end up on your couch, binging the latest series instead? This is where the real magic of like-mindedness comes into play. You're not alone in your procrastination; in fact, you've got a whole squad cheering you on from their respective sofa kingdoms. This shared experience can be both hilarious and frustrating. We've all been there—promising ourselves that "tomorrow will be different," while simultaneously setting our alarms for the latest binge-watching marathon. The first step to breaking free from this loop is acknowledging that we're all stuck in it together, and maybe, just maybe, we can motivate each other to rise from the depths of our Netflix cocoons.

Now, let's talk about clutter. If you've ever tried to find something in your room only to discover a forgotten snack from three months ago, you know the struggle is real. The comfort of like-mindedness extends to our shared love for disorganization, as we collectively navigate our messy lives. There's something strangely bonding about showing up to a meeting with a coffee stain on your shirt and receipts spilling out of your bag. It's like a badge of honor in our chaotic lives, but deep down, we know it's time for a change. Embracing minimalism can be a revolutionary step, but it's much easier when you realize that your friends are just as overwhelmed by clutter. Maybe tackling the mess together will turn into a hilarious group activity rather than a dreaded chore.

Finally, let's circle back to mental health. In a world where anxiety often feels like the default setting, finding comfort in like-mindedness can be a double-edged sword. Yes, it's nice to know others share your struggles, but it's equally vital to uplift one another toward positive habits. Instead of wallowing in our collective anxiety, let's create a supportive environment where we can swap tips on sleep hygiene, exercise routines, and healthy eating habits. Who knows? We might just inspire each other to turn our comfort zones into growth zones, one awkwardly shared smoothie recipe at a time. After all, if we can find humor in our shared chaos, maybe we can also find the strength to move forward together.

Challenging Your Inner Circle

Challenging your inner circle can feel like trying to convince a cat to take a bath – messy, chaotic, and likely to end with someone hissing. But if you're surrounded by friends who treat junk food like it's a food group and spend more time scrolling through memes than actually living life, it's time to reevaluate. Your inner circle should be your support team, not a group of enablers who encourage doomscrolling and binge-watching shows until the sun comes up. So, grab your metaphorical boxing gloves and let's dive into the challenge of upgrading your crew.

First, let's face the music: if your friends are more invested in TikTok dances than in building a future, you might want to consider swapping out a few of those dance partners. Surrounding yourself with people who share your goals can create a powerful ripple effect. It's like a gym buddy, but instead of spotting you while you lift weights, they're spotting you while you lift your spirits and ambitions. Think of it as a friendship makeover; instead of letting negativity drag you down like a heavy backpack full of textbooks, you can lighten the load with friends who inspire you to take that first step towards growth.

Next, we need to tackle the echo chambers. If your group chats consist of endless rants about how life is totally unfair or how the latest Netflix series is the pinnacle of human achievement, it's time for a change. Challenge each other to break out of those cycles. Suggest a book club – yes, actual books! – or create a "No Doomscroll" day where everyone agrees to put down their phones and do something productive. You might even discover that there's life beyond the screen. Who knew, right? It might feel like stepping into the unknown, but it could be a refreshing break from the same old scroll-fest.

Now, let's talk about the clutter—not just the physical kind, but the mental chaos that comes from hanging out with the wrong crowd. If your space resembles a tornado aftermath and your brain feels like it's stuck in a perpetual to-do list, it's high time for some decluttering. Start by removing toxic influences from your life, be it friends who always choose the couch over the gym or those who think "healthy eating" means ordering a salad with extra ranch dressing. Surround yourself with people who value organization and motivation, and who encourage you to tackle that never-ending list of goals. You'll be amazed at how much easier it is to move forward when your circle is pushing you in the right direction.

Lastly, embrace the beauty of boundaries. It's perfectly okay to tell your friends that you're focusing on your health, productivity, or even just trying to get a full eight hours of sleep without the allure of late-night snack sessions. It's like saying no to that last slice of pizza when you know you've already had three. Set clear expectations with your inner circle; let them know you're on a mission to become a better version of yourself. After all, if they're truly your friends, they'll respect your journey and maybe even join in on the fun. Who knows? You might end up creating a whole new squad dedicated to health, happiness, and getting things done – one small step at a time.

In conclusion, challenging your inner circle is a journey worth taking. It's about finding those who uplift you, support your goals, and encourage you to embrace positive habits. So, go forth and be the change you want to see in your friendships. With a little humor, a sprinkle of motivation, and a dash of courage, you can transform your inner circle into a powerhouse of positivity. Remember, life is too short to get stuck in an inertia loop of junk food and negativity. It's time to step up, step out, and surround yourself with the people who will help you move forward.

Seeking Diverse Perspectives

Imagine you're scrolling through social media, and every post seems to echo your own thoughts. You're caught in a cozy little bubble where everyone thinks just like you. Sounds nice, right? Well, it might be time to pop that bubble! Seeking diverse perspectives is like adding sprinkles to your boring vanilla ice cream; it turns a monotonous scoop into a delightful sundae. Embracing different viewpoints not only widens your understanding of the world but also helps you escape the doomscrolling trap. After all, who wants to spend hours staring at the same old opinions when there's a whole buffet of ideas just waiting to be tasted?

Diving into diverse perspectives can feel a bit like trying to eat vegetables when you've been chowing down on junk food your whole life. At first, it may seem uncomfortable and not quite as appealing. However, just like that kale smoothie you reluctantly swallowed, exposing yourself to other viewpoints can be surprisingly refreshing. Whether it's engaging with someone from a different background, reading books outside your usual genre, or even tuning into podcasts that challenge your beliefs, it's essential to step outside your comfort zone. Trust me, your brain will thank you later, and you might just discover a new favorite flavor of thought.

Now, let's address the elephant in the room—echo chambers. These are the cozy corners of the internet where your thoughts are validated and your biases are reinforced. While it feels great to have your opinions paraded around, it's worth considering that this can lead to a serious case of intellectual constipation. When you only consume information that aligns with your views, you risk becoming stagnant and uninformed. So, shake things up! Find a friend who loves to debate or join a group that thrives on divergent opinions. It's like adding a splash of hot sauce to your bland diet; it may sting a little, but it's all about the flavor!

Speaking of flavor, how about we spice up our daily routines while we're at it? A sprinkle of variety can do wonders for that inertia loop we often find ourselves trapped in. It's easy to fall into the routine of scrolling, snacking, and snoozing your way through life. However, by intentionally seeking out different perspectives—whether through documentaries, attending workshops, or even participating in community events—you can create a dynamic and engaging day-to-day experience. Consider it a buffet of ideas where you can mix and match to create your own unique dish. Who knows? You might even discover a new hobby or passion that propels you forward!

In the grand scheme of things, seeking diverse perspectives is not just a feel-good activity; it's a crucial ingredient for personal growth. Life is not a straight line, and sometimes you need a detour to appreciate the scenery. By embracing a variety of viewpoints, you can improve your mental resilience, break the cycle of negativity, and declutter that overwhelmed mind of yours. So, the next time you find yourself in a scrolling stupor or munching on the same old thoughts, remember: there's a whole world of flavors out there waiting for you to dig in. Get out there, explore, and let the diversity of perspectives be the fuel that propels you into a more fulfilling life!

Move Forward: Building Healthy Habits for a Fulfilling Life

Chapter 3: Junk Food and the Standard American Diet

The Temptation of Fast Food

The allure of fast food is like a siren song for many of us, especially when life feels like a never-ending treadmill of chaos. Picture this: you've had a long day filled with meetings, errands, and a constant battle against the clock. Your stomach growls louder than an angry toddler, and suddenly, the golden arches or the bell that rings just for you seem like the best thing since sliced bread—or at least sliced fries. Fast food is marketed as the ultimate convenience, promising a delicious escape from the whirlwind of responsibilities. But let's be real; it's more like a trapdoor into the abyss of regret and a diet that would make a nutritionist weep.

Fast food chains have mastered the art of distraction, much like those endless scrolls through social media that leave you questioning your life choices. The flashy ads and irresistible deals are designed to pull you in faster than a cat chasing a laser pointer. You know what I'm talking about: "Buy one, get one free!" Suddenly, you're not just hungry; you're a savvy consumer on a mission. But what they don't tell you is that this mission often leads to a post-meal slump that feels like you've just run a marathon—while wearing a potato sack.

And let's address the elephant in the room: the Standard American Diet. This diet could easily be rebranded as the "Why Am I So Tired?" diet. Fast food often plays a starring role, loaded with sugars, fats, and enough sodium to make a salt shaker blush. Sure, it's quick and cheap, but it's also a one-way ticket to feeling sluggish and cranky. When you combine that with doomscrolling through the latest viral trends, you've got the perfect recipe for spiraling anxiety and feeling perpetually overwhelmed. Who needs an emotional rollercoaster when you can just grab a burger and call it a day?

Now, if you're thinking, "But it's just food, and I'm busy!" let's not kid ourselves. Eating junk food is like putting a Band-Aid on a gaping wound; it might feel good for a moment, but it's not doing you any favors in the long run. You might think you're saving time, but what you're really doing is gifting yourself a side of guilt, poor sleep, and an even longer to-do list. The key to moving forward lies in building healthy habits, like meal prepping or whipping up a quick stir-fry, which can be done in less time than it takes to wait in line for that drive-thru.

Ultimately, the temptation of fast food is a battle we all face, but it doesn't have to end in defeat. Embracing mindful eating can help you reclaim your time and your health. So the next time you find yourself in a crunch, remember that taking a few minutes to prepare a wholesome meal can do wonders for your mood, energy, and goal-crushing abilities. Instead of succumbing to the clutches of convenience, why not make a pact with yourself to find joy in the kitchen, even if it means starting with a microwave meal that doesn't come from a clown? It's all about progress, not perfection, as you move forward to a fulfilling life.

Reading Labels: A Life Skill

Reading labels is like a secret dance with your food, and trust me, it's more entertaining than scrolling through social media for the hundredth time. You might think that deciphering those tiny, cryptic letters is akin to reading ancient hieroglyphics, but fear not! Once you crack the code, it becomes your superpower in the battle against the standard American diet, which, let's be honest, often resembles a junk food circus. Instead of munching on whatever your favorite algorithm suggests, you can strut confidently into the grocery store, ready to make informed choices that will make both your taste buds and your body happy.

First, let's talk about the ingredients list. It's a bit like people watching at a party: you want to know who's who and what they're all about. If you see a bunch of ingredients you can't pronounce, it's probably time to wave goodbye and find something more wholesome. When you spot items like "high fructose corn syrup" or "artificial flavors," consider them the party crashers of your diet. They may look flashy, but they're really just here to sabotage your health goals. Instead, seek out whole ingredients that sound less like a science project and more like something you'd find in your grandma's kitchen.

Now, let's dive into serving sizes. This is where the fun really begins! The serving size on the label may be a mere suggestion, but it's often a sneaky little trick. Think of it like a movie trailer that shows all the best parts but leaves out the boring details. That tiny "one serving" might just make you feel like you're in a diet horror film, where one serving is gone in three bites. So, next time you pick up a bag of chips, remember: just because the label says one serving is twelve chips doesn't mean you can't eat the whole bag. (Okay, maybe not the whole bag, but you get the point!)

Then we have the nutrition facts, which are essentially the report card for your food. Look for fiber, protein, and healthy fats— they're like the A-students of the nutrition world. They'll keep you full and energized, unlike those sugar-laden snacks that leave you feeling like you just crashed your car into a wall. And don't forget about sugars! If you see "added sugars," it's like a neon sign flashing, "RUN AWAY!" Your body doesn't need that kind of drama, especially when you're already juggling work, social life, and possibly a Netflix binge.

Finally, let's not overlook the power of your choices. Reading labels is not just about what you eat; it's about reclaiming control over your life. When you start making informed decisions at the grocery store, you're not just choosing food; you're choosing to move forward. It's a life skill that empowers you to break free from doomscrolling and the echo chambers of negativity. So, the next time you feel overwhelmed or lost, remember that reading labels is like having a roadmap to a healthier you. With a bit of humor and a dash of determination, you can turn this simple task into a personal victory, one label at a time.

Cooking Healthy: It's Not Rocket Science

Cooking healthy is like riding a bike: wobbly at first, but once you find your balance, it's a smooth ride that gets easier with practice. Yes, the idea of whipping up a nutritious meal after a long day can feel as appealing as watching paint dry. But here's the good news—cooking healthy isn't a secret science experiment that requires a PhD in foodology. It's about making simple choices that don't involve a microwave or a takeout menu. So grab your spatula and let's dive into the delicious world of not-so-complicated cooking.

First, let's tackle the common misconception that healthy eating involves endless hours of chopping vegetables and measuring quinoa like you're preparing for a NASA mission. Spoiler alert: you don't need to be a culinary genius to create meals that won't make your taste buds cry. Start with the basics—think of meals that resemble your favorite childhood snacks, but with a nutritious twist. Swap out potato chips for air-popped popcorn sprinkled with a hint of salt, or trade that sugary cereal for a bowl of oatmeal topped with fruits and nuts. It's all about finding healthier alternatives that keep your cravings satisfied without sending your body into a sugar coma.

Now, let's talk about the kitchen's best-kept secrets: frozen veggies and canned beans. If fresh produce intimidates you like a pop quiz, fear not! Those frozen veggies are just waiting to be tossed into a skillet and made to feel fancy with a dash of olive oil and some garlic. And canned beans? They're like the superheroes of the pantry—packed with protein, fiber, and the ability to turn any blah dish into a hearty meal. You can literally dump them into a salad or blend them into a soup and call it gourmet. Who knew healthy cooking could be so easy, right?

One of the biggest hurdles in cooking healthy is the dreaded "I don't have time" mantra. But here's a little secret: meal prep is your new best friend. Spend a couple of hours on the weekend chopping, cooking, and storing meals in handy containers, and you're setting yourself up for success. This way, when the dreaded "What's for dinner?" question arises after a long day, you'll have a delicious answer ready to go. Imagine the satisfaction of opening your fridge and finding a colorful, prepped meal instead of a sad, wilted piece of lettuce. It's a game changer!

Finally, let's get real about the joy of cooking. It doesn't have to be a chore; it can be a creative outlet and a way to unwind. Put on your favorite playlist, channel your inner chef, and have some fun experimenting in the kitchen. Start small, maybe with a simple stir-fry that allows you to throw in whatever you have lying around. And if it doesn't turn out as expected? Embrace the chaos! Remember, cooking healthy isn't rocket science; it's all about making choices and enjoying the journey. So roll up those sleeves and get cooking—your body and taste buds will thank you!

Chapter 4: The Negativity Trap

Identifying Negative Thought Patterns

Identifying negative thought patterns is akin to finding that one rogue sock that mysteriously appears in the laundry—unexpected, annoying, and ultimately a sign that something's amiss. We all have those moments where our minds go on a wild trip through the worst-case scenario forest, where every tree is a new worry. It's like the brain has its own horror movie playing on repeat, and we're the captive audience, munching on popcorn while doomscrolling through social media. Instead of enjoying the show, we need to learn how to change the channel, and that starts with identifying those pesky negative thoughts that hold us back.

First, let's talk about the echo chamber. You know, that delightful place where your thoughts bounce around like a ping-pong ball, but instead of fun, it just reinforces your worries. If you find yourself trapped in a cycle where you only hear what you want to hear—like "I can't do this" or "I'll never be successful"—it's time to break out the mental sledgehammer. Challenge those thoughts! Ask yourself, "Is this really true, or am I just being dramatic?" Spoiler alert: you're probably being dramatic. Remember, every superhero has their kryptonite, and negative thoughts are yours. The trick is to identify them before they sabotage your mission to move forward.

Next up, let's tackle the "Inertia Loop." Sounds fancy, right? It's basically when you find yourself in a comfortable rut, binge-watching yet another series instead of tackling that to-do list. It's like your brain is stuck in a low-energy hamster wheel, and you're just along for the ride. To escape this loop, start by identifying what thoughts keep you stuck. Are you telling yourself, "I'll start tomorrow"? Well, newsflash: tomorrow is a mythical creature that never seems to arrive. Instead, set small, manageable goals—like doing just one task. Soon enough, you'll find that the inertia has turned into momentum, and you'll be zooming past those Netflix credits.

Another sneaky negative thought pattern is the "Comparison Trap." Social media can be a slippery slope, filled with carefully curated lives that make you feel like you're still in your pajamas at noon (spoiler: you probably are). When you start to feel less-than, remind yourself that those influencers are likely just as lost as you are, possibly even wearing the same pajamas! Focus on your own journey instead of scrolling through someone else's highlight reel. Celebrate your small wins, even if that means finally making your bed or resisting the siren call of junk food for a day. You're not in a race; you're building your own unique path forward.

Lastly, let's address the "Dopamine Dilemma." In a world where instant gratification is a click away, it's easy to fall into the trap of seeking quick hits of happiness through junk food, mindless scrolling, or that fifth episode of a show you really didn't need to watch. These habits can create a cycle of anxiety and stress, leaving you feeling overwhelmed and unproductive. Recognize that while it's great to enjoy these things, true satisfaction comes from building healthy habits that promote long-term well-being. Start small—replace one unhealthy snack with a piece of fruit, or set a timer for 20 minutes of focused work followed by a 5-minute break. Trust me, your future self will thank you.

Practicing Gratitude: It's Not Just for Thanksgiving

Practicing gratitude isn't just for the pumpkin pie enthusiasts or those who find themselves awkwardly holding hands in a circle before carving the turkey. It's a powerful tool that can help even the busiest of us, whether you're juggling five responsibilities, scrolling through social media like it's a competitive sport, or trying to remember the last time you drank water instead of coffee. Imagine trading in your doomscrolling habit for a gratitude practice. Sounds revolutionary, right? Instead of getting lost in a rabbit hole of negativity, you could be reflecting on what's actually going right in your life, like the fact that you survived another week without burning your dinner or that Wi-Fi is still working.

Think about it: when was the last time you took a moment to appreciate something simple? Maybe it was that perfect slice of pizza or the rare moment when you found a matching pair of socks. Gratitude has this magical way of shifting our focus from what we're lacking to what we already have. It's like putting on a pair of rose-colored glasses, but instead of seeing the world through a filter, you're seeing it through a lens of appreciation. Even during those chaotic days when your to-do list looks like it was written by a caffeinated octopus, taking 30 seconds to acknowledge something good can be a game changer. So, let's put down the junk food for a sec and consider how a gratitude practice can help us make sense of the chaos.

For those feeling perpetually lost, gratitude can act as a compass. You might think, "What do I have to be grateful for? My life is a mess!" But here's the kicker: it's usually in the mess where we find the most profound moments of gratitude. Perhaps you're grateful for the friends who tolerate your existential crises or the fact that you can still binge-watch your favorite shows after a long day. Recognizing these small victories can help you climb out of that inertia loop and spark a little motivation to tackle those goals you've been putting off. Plus, who wouldn't feel a little lighter after realizing you're one meme away from a good laugh?

Now, let's address the elephant in the room—time (or lack thereof). Between work, social life, and trying to remember if you've eaten in the last 24 hours, it can feel impossible to squeeze in gratitude. But here's a pro tip: gratitude doesn't require a dedicated hour. It can be as simple as jotting down three things you're thankful for while waiting for your coffee to brew or during your "what-am-I-doing-with-my-life" shower thoughts. It's like a cheat code for your brain that helps you reset from stress and overwhelm back to a state of calm and clarity, which is ideal for those of us who feel like we're perpetually running on empty.

In the end, practicing gratitude isn't just a seasonal activity; it's a lifelong investment in your happiness and well-being. By actively engaging in gratitude, you're choosing to prioritize positivity over the clutter of negativity that life throws at you. So, the next time you find yourself spiraling into an echo chamber of despair or facing a pile of clutter that could rival a small mountain, take a moment to reflect on what's good in your life. Whether it's the cozy sweater you found in the back of your closet or the fact that you didn't trip while walking down the street today, celebrate those little wins. After all, living a fulfilling life is all about moving forward—one grateful thought at a time.

Surrounding Yourself with Positivity

Surrounding yourself with positivity is like trying to cultivate a garden in a junkyard; it might seem impossible at first, but with a little effort, you can turn that mess into a flourishing paradise. First off, let's talk about the delightful world of doomscrolling. If you've ever found yourself knee-deep in a rabbit hole of bad news and cat memes at 3 AM, you know what I mean. It's time to put down the smartphone and step away from the abyss. Instead of allowing algorithms to dictate your mood, curate your digital environment like you would a playlist. Replace that endless scroll with uplifting stories, engaging podcasts, or even a good ol' book. Who knew your phone could be a source of joy rather than just a portal to anxiety?

Now, let's tackle the echo chambers. Think of it like this: if you only listen to your favorite band on repeat, you might miss out on discovering that hidden gem of a song that could change your life. Surrounding yourself with diverse perspectives is key to expanding your mental horizons. Engage in conversations with people who challenge your views—yes, even that one friend who insists pineapple belongs on pizza. You'll find that embracing a variety of opinions can lead to growth and a more nuanced understanding of the world. Plus, it's a great way to practice your debate skills for when you inevitably need to convince your friends that "Friends" is the best show of all time.

Next on the positivity train is nutrition, which is often overlooked when discussing mental well-being. Eating junk food might feel good in the moment, but it's like trying to fuel a sports car with soda and gummy bears. Instead, think of your body as a high-performance vehicle that needs premium fuel. Incorporate colorful fruits and vegetables into your diet, and watch as your energy levels soar, making it easier to tackle that never-ending to-do list. And yes, sneaking in a piece of chocolate now and then is perfectly acceptable; even Ferraris need a little fun sometimes.

Speaking of to-do lists, let's address the dreaded inertia loop. It's like being stuck in quicksand—once you're in, it feels nearly impossible to escape. The secret is to start small. Set achievable goals like organizing one drawer or taking a five-minute stretch break. Celebrate these tiny victories like you just won an Olympic gold medal. Over time, you'll build momentum, and before you know it, you'll be on a roll, tackling bigger tasks with ease. Just remember, every great journey begins with a single step, even if that step is just getting out of bed and putting on pants.

Finally, let's chat about clutter and organization. If your room looks like a tornado hit a thrift store, it's time for a makeover. Decluttering isn't just about tidying up; it's about creating a sanctuary where positivity can thrive. Take a few minutes each day to clear out the junk, and you'll be amazed at how your mental clarity improves. Plus, a clean space can do wonders for your sleep quality, allowing you to tackle life's challenges with renewed energy. After all, a positive environment fosters a positive mindset, and who doesn't want to feel like a superhero in their own life?

Chapter 5: The Daily Routine: Friend or Foe?

Creating a Routine That Works for You

Creating a routine that works for you is like finding the perfect pair of socks: it requires some trial and error, a bit of patience, and maybe a few mismatched moments along the way. First off, let's address the elephant in the room—your smartphone. It's not just a phone; it's a black hole of doomscrolling and endless TikTok dances. If your idea of a productive day includes watching cat videos for hours, it's time to reclaim your time. Start by setting specific times to check your social media, because, believe it or not, those influencers aren't going anywhere. You'll be surprised at how much time you can free up when you're not scrolling through endless memes.

Next, let's talk about food. If your diet consists mainly of snacks that come in crinkly bags and are designed to be eaten in one sitting, you might want to rethink your choices. Creating a routine around healthy eating doesn't have to mean turning into a kale-chomping rabbit. Start small—maybe swap out one junk food item for something that actually resembles food. Think of it as a culinary adventure with a side of health benefits. Plus, your body will thank you when it stops feeling like a circus tent stuffed with cotton candy.

For those of you who feel like you're trapped in an inertia loop, it's time to shake things up. Start your day with one simple task— maybe making your bed or pouring that first cup of coffee. Completing a small action can give you the boost you need to tackle bigger goals. It's like giving your brain a little high five. Once you've accomplished that task, you might find the motivation to tackle more. And hey, if it takes five cups of coffee to get you there, who's judging?

Now, let's address the clutter situation. Whether it's your bedroom resembling a tornado aftermath or your desk looking like a paper monster exploded, decluttering is key. Set aside just fifteen minutes a day to tackle one small area. It's amazing what you can accomplish in a short burst of chaos control. Plus, you'll be amazed at what you find—like that missing sock or the remote control that's been MIA for weeks. A tidy space can lead to a tidy mind, and who wouldn't want that?

Lastly, don't underestimate the power of sleep. A good night's sleep can turn a grumpy gremlin into a functioning human. Establish a bedtime routine that doesn't involve scrolling through your phone until your eyelids weigh a ton. Instead, try reading a book or practicing a bit of mindfulness. Your future self will thank you when you wake up feeling like a well-rested superhero ready to conquer the day. Remember, creating a routine that works for you is all about finding what fits, making adjustments, and laughing at the messes along the way. So go ahead, get started, and embrace the beautiful chaos of life!

The Power of Small Habits

Small habits might seem like the underdogs of the self-improvement world, but don't let their size fool you. They pack a punch! Imagine trying to lift a giant weight at the gym without ever doing a single push-up. Spoiler alert: you're going to flop harder than a pancake on a Sunday morning. Small habits are like those little push-ups. They're manageable, and when you do them consistently, they transform into something mighty. Instead of trying to overhaul your entire life in one fell swoop, why not start with something as simple as drinking a glass of water first thing in the morning? Your body will thank you, and you'll feel less like a soggy sponge.

Now, let's talk about doomscrolling. You know, that delightful activity where you swipe through social media like it's a never-ending buffet of negativity? Instead of consuming every morsel of bad news, how about swapping that time for a five-minute walk? It's like hitting the refresh button on your mental browser. The world isn't going to end because you missed a meme or two, and you'll find that stepping away from the screen can clear up more than just your vision. Plus, fresh air is like a free mood booster. Who knew that nature had a better Wi-Fi connection than your phone?

For those of you who find yourselves in the clutches of junk food, listen up! We're not saying you need to ditch your favorite snacks entirely, but how about adding a small habit of munching on an apple or a carrot stick before diving into those nachos? It's like giving your body a gentle reminder that it can handle some real food before the processed stuff. You'll be surprised how these small choices can shift your cravings. Before you know it, you might be sharing stories about how you once survived a week without a soda—like a modern-day hero!

Let's tackle the inertia loop, shall we? That glorious cycle of procrastination where you find yourself binge-watching a show about people who are also procrastinating. Instead of waiting for inspiration to strike like lightning, try setting a timer for just five minutes to start that chore you've been avoiding. It's like tricking your brain into thinking, "Hey, it's just five minutes! I can totally do that!" Spoiler alert: once you get started, you often keep going. It's the classic "just one more episode" dilemma, but this time, it's about accomplishing something instead of just scrolling mindlessly.

Finally, let's not forget about sleep hygiene. We've all heard that sleep is important, but do you really need to scroll through memes at 2 AM? Instead of counting sheep, how about implementing a small bedtime routine? Try reading a book, or even better, put your phone in another room. Trust us, the world won't implode if you miss a few late-night TikToks. With some small adjustments, you'll wake up feeling more refreshed than a can of soda after a long day in the sun. So, embrace those small habits. They're the secret sauce to moving forward, and who doesn't want to be a superhero in their own life?

Breaking Free from Boredom

Boredom is like that uninvited guest who crashes your party, eats all the snacks, and refuses to leave. It creeps up on you when you least expect it, especially when you find yourself scrolling endlessly through social media, falling into the black hole of doomscrolling. You know the drill: one minute, you're checking for the latest meme, and the next, you're knee-deep in conspiracy theories about the moon landing. Breaking free from this digital quagmire is crucial if you want to reclaim your time and sanity. Instead of scrolling through the same old algorithmically curated nonsense, how about diving into something that genuinely sparks your interest? Read a book, pick up a new hobby, or even watch a documentary that doesn't involve TikTok dances. Trust me, your brain will thank you.

Now, let's talk about food because, let's face it, we've all had those late-night snacks that make us question our life choices. The standard American diet is like a buffet of bad decisions, and eating junk food is way too easy. But here's a thought: what if you treated your body like a sports car instead of a clunker? You wouldn't fuel a Lamborghini with expired gas, right? So, why not try whipping up a quick, healthy meal instead of inhaling a bag of chips? You'll not only feel better, but you might even impress yourself with your culinary skills. Who knows? You might just discover a hidden talent for making the perfect avocado toast.

When you're feeling overwhelmed, it's easy to slip into a negative mindset, which is like putting on a pair of glasses that only show the worst in life. Instead of letting negativity take the wheel, grab a metaphorical steering wheel and drive your thoughts towards something more positive. Gratitude journals are all the rage, and for good reason! Spending just a few minutes each day noting what you're thankful for can flip your perspective faster than you can say "I need coffee." And hey, if writing isn't your thing, try talking to a friend or blasting your favorite playlist. Just don't forget to dance like nobody's watching; it's therapeutic, trust me.

Organization—let's face it, it's a word that can trigger anxiety in even the most laid-back individuals. If your room looks like a tornado hit it, it's time to channel your inner Marie Kondo and declutter. Start small: tackle one corner of your room or your desk, and soon you'll find yourself feeling lighter than a helium balloon. Plus, a tidy space can do wonders for your mental clarity. You'll be amazed at how much more motivated you feel when you're not stumbling over yesterday's laundry or searching for your missing sock. And while you're at it, create a daily routine that doesn't leave you feeling like you're in a hamster wheel.

Finally, let's talk about movement. No, you don't have to run a marathon or become a gym rat; just find ways to incorporate activity into your day. Dance around your living room, take a brisk walk while listening to your favorite podcast, or try a quick workout video online. The goal isn't to become an Olympic athlete overnight; it's about breaking the inertia loop that keeps you stuck in a sedentary lifestyle. And remember, sleep is your best friend. Prioritize it like you would a hot date; after all, a well-rested brain is a productive brain. By tackling boredom with creativity, positivity, organization, and a sprinkle of movement, you'll not only break free from the mundane but also pave the way for a fulfilling life.

Chapter 6: Goal Setting and the Art of Not Accomplishing

Setting SMART Goals: Not Just for Business People

Setting SMART goals is like trying to get a cat to take a bath—challenging, but oh-so-rewarding if you can pull it off. The acronym stands for Specific, Measurable, Achievable, Relevant, and Time-bound. Now, before you roll your eyes and think this is just some corporate mumbo-jumbo meant for people in suits, let's break it down for everyone—yes, even for those who can't remember where they left their phone. Setting SMART goals can help you climb out of the doomscrolling abyss and dodge the algorithms that seem to know your snack preferences better than you do.

Let's start with Specific. Imagine you want to eat healthier. Instead of saying, "I want to eat better," try, "I will eat three servings of vegetables every day." That's a specific goal! You've just told your brain what you want to achieve. It's like giving your brain a GPS instead of a vague map that leads to a drive-thru. Being specific helps you avoid the echo chambers of negativity and junk food that often crowd your mind.

Next up is Measurable. If you can't measure it, did it even happen? Saying you'll "exercise more" is as useful as saying you'll "do better" in life. Instead, set a measurable goal like, "I will walk 10,000 steps a day." Now you can track your progress and hold yourself accountable. Plus, it gives you something to brag about to your friends, like how you conquered that pesky couch potato phase.

Achievable is where many people trip up. Setting lofty goals like "I will become a world-renowned chef by next week" is just setting yourself up for a faceplant. Instead, aim for something realistic, like cooking one new healthy recipe each week. This way, you can gradually build your culinary skills without adding to the clutter of your kitchen. It's a great way to avoid feeling overwhelmed and to keep your mental health in check.

Now, let's talk about Relevance. This is where you ask yourself if your goal actually matters to you. If you're setting goals because your friend is doing it or because some Instagram influencer told you to, it's time to rethink your strategy. A relevant goal might be, "I want to read one book a month to improve my focus." This ties in neatly with your desire to grow and move forward, instead of getting lost in the chaos of daily life. Lastly, don't forget the Time-bound part. Without a deadline, your goal is just a wish. Set a timeframe like, "I will complete my book by the end of the month." And just like that, you've set yourself up for a win, giving you a sense of accomplishment amidst the stress of life!

Celebrating Small Wins: Confetti Optional

In the grand journey of life, it's easy to feel like you need a parade for every accomplishment, but let's face it: confetti can be messy, and who has time for cleaning up after a celebration when you're already juggling a million things? Celebrating small wins doesn't require a full-blown fiesta. Sometimes, all it takes is a mental high-five or a little dance in your living room. Whether you finally organized that sock drawer which had been a black hole of mismatched socks or managed to resist the siren call of your phone while scrolling through social media, these small victories deserve recognition. They're like tiny stepping stones on the path to a more fulfilling life, and trust us, those stones are way less slippery than they sound.

Imagine you've just completed a task that's been on your to-do list longer than your last haircut. Instead of drowning in self-doubt or doomscrolling for validation, take a moment to bask in the glory of your achievement. Whether you've eaten a proper meal instead of snacking on the last remnants of yesterday's pizza or finally tackled the clutter that's been confusing your cat, give yourself a pat on the back. Celebrating these small wins can help break the inertia loop that keeps you stuck in a cycle of procrastination. It's like giving your brain a little dopamine hit without the need for a sugar crash later.

You might wonder, how do I celebrate without turning my living room into a scene from a party planning show? The secret is simplicity. Instead of throwing a confetti-covered bash, how about treating yourself to your favorite snack or taking a moment to just breathe? Maybe even watch an episode of that show you've been meaning to catch up on. You could also try writing down your achievements in a journal. This not only helps you track your progress but also allows you to look back at all the small wins when you're feeling lost in the chaos of life. Remember, a little recognition goes a long way in building confidence and momentum.

Now, let's talk about the power of positive reinforcement. When you acknowledge your small wins, you're training your brain to look for the good amidst the clutter of negativity that often surrounds us. In a world filled with echo chambers and algorithms that thrive on our attention, it's easy to get sucked into a vortex of despair. But by celebrating those small victories, you're essentially thumbing your nose at the negativity and saying, "I'm not going down without a fight!" Plus, the more you recognize these wins, the easier it becomes to keep building healthy habits and routines. It's like a snowball effect, but instead of rolling downhill into a mess, you're creating a delightful snowman of positivity.

Lastly, celebrating small wins can serve as a reminder that growth doesn't always come in giant leaps. For those of you feeling overwhelmed by the pressures of adulting, remember that every step counts. Whether it's choosing a salad over fries or finally getting around to folding that laundry (which, let's be honest, has been a mountain in the corner of your room), give yourself credit. Life is a series of small victories strung together, and by celebrating them, you're crafting a narrative of resilience and progress. So, the next time you find yourself staring at that daunting to-do list, just remember: confetti is optional, but a little self-celebration is essential.

Overcoming the Inertia Loop

Have you ever found yourself scrolling through your phone, a snack in one hand, and wondering how you ended up in the depths of a cat video rabbit hole? Welcome to the inertia loop, where time flies faster than a caffeine-fueled squirrel, and your goals seem to vanish like your willpower around junk food. Breaking out of this loop can feel like trying to lift a couch with one hand—awkward, messy, and likely to end in a faceplant. But fear not! With a sprinkle of humor and a dash of determination, we can kick that inertia to the curb and start moving forward.

First things first: identify the culprits of your inertia. Is it that never-ending scroll through social media, or perhaps the lure of that well-deserved couch potato lifestyle? Maybe it's the delicious siren call of a bag of chips? Acknowledge these distractions as the mischievous gremlins they are. Instead of allowing them to control your life, treat them like that one friend who always convinces you to binge-watch another episode, and then suddenly it's 2 AM. Set boundaries! Try using apps that limit your screen time or designate a specific "snack time" so those potato chips don't become your best pals.

Next, let's talk routines. The word "routine" might make you think of your high school math teacher droning on about algebra, but trust me, creating a daily routine can be more exciting than it sounds. Think of it as your personal superhero cape! Start small: wake up, stretch, drink a glass of water, and voilà! You've already accomplished more before breakfast than most people do all day. Gradually add in activities that align with your goals. Want to exercise? Walk in place while you catch up on your favorite show. It's multitasking at its finest and a great way to show those calories who's boss.

Decluttering your space is another crucial step in overcoming inertia. You'd be surprised how a clean room can lift your mood faster than a double espresso. Start by tossing out one item each day. It could be that ancient pizza box or that T-shirt from high school that no longer fits—because let's be real, we've all been there. Once you clear the clutter, you'll find it's easier to think clearly and focus on what really matters. Plus, you'll impress your mom when she drops by unannounced and doesn't have to step over your laundry mountain.

Lastly, let's tackle the elephant in the room: mental health. It's okay to feel overwhelmed. We all have days when our brains feel like they're stuck in molasses. Implement mindfulness techniques like deep breathing or guided meditation apps—no, they won't magically solve all your problems, but they can help clear some mental fog. Combine this with good sleep hygiene, and you'll be surprised at how much clearer your mind becomes. Remember, good sleep is not just a luxury; it's a necessity for fighting off that inertia.

In summary, overcoming the inertia loop doesn't have to be a daunting task. By recognizing your distractions, establishing a routine, decluttering your space, and prioritizing your mental health, you can step out of the chaos and into a more fulfilling life. And who knows? You might even find time to enjoy a cat video or two—just not at the expense of your goals! So lace up those sneakers, grab a water bottle, and let's move forward with humor and purpose.

Chapter 7: Clutter: The Silent Saboteur

Why Messiness Matters

Messiness is often seen as a problem to be solved, a chaotic monster lurking in the corners of our bedrooms, offices, and minds. But what if I told you that embracing a little messiness could actually be a game-changer on your journey to building healthy habits? Think of it as the messy friend who shows up at the party uninvited but ends up being the life of it. Instead of constantly battling the clutter of your physical and mental space, consider how that very clutter might hold the key to your growth, creativity, and, dare I say, happiness.

In a world where social media algorithms are like that one overly enthusiastic friend who insists on showing you the same meme 50 times, it's easy to get trapped in echo chambers and negativity loops. But messiness can be a breath of fresh air! It challenges us to break free from our routines and invites spontaneity. That pile of laundry you've been avoiding? It's not just a reminder of your procrastination; it's a potential treasure trove of creativity. You might find that shirt you forgot you had, which could inspire a whole new outfit or a dance party in your living room. Embracing messiness gives you the freedom to explore, play, and laugh at yourself a little along the way.

Life can be overwhelming, especially when you're juggling work, studies, social obligations, and that endless to-do list that seems to multiply faster than rabbits. Enter the world of messiness, where the chaos can actually spark productivity. When you stop trying to be the poster child for perfect organization, you might just discover that messiness can lead to breakthroughs. Maybe that cluttered desk has the notes you need for your next big project or the last slice of pizza (don't pretend it's not in there). Allowing for some disorganization can create a space for ideas to flourish and for you to tackle tasks one chaotic step at a time.

And let's not forget the role of messiness in self-acceptance. In a society that often glorifies perfection, it's easy to feel like you're falling short. But guess what? Everyone is messy in one way or another. Whether it's a chaotic schedule or a fridge filled with questionable leftovers, embracing your messiness can lead to a sense of camaraderie with others who are also trying to figure it all out. It's a reminder that you're not alone in this wild ride called life. Plus, when you allow yourself to be imperfect, you give others permission to do the same, creating a ripple effect of authenticity and connection.

So, next time you find yourself feeling anxious or overwhelmed, take a moment to appreciate the mess. Whether it's a cluttered workspace or a few unmade decisions, remember that messiness is not the enemy—it's a quirky companion on your journey to building healthy habits. Instead of viewing mess as a hindrance, see it as an opportunity to laugh, learn, and grow. Embrace the chaos, find joy in the imperfect, and watch as your life becomes a little more colorful and a lot more fulfilling.

Decluttering Your Space, Decluttering Your Mind

Decluttering your space is like giving your brain a much-needed vacation. Imagine your mind as a cluttered attic filled with forgotten treasures, dust bunnies, and the occasional existential crisis. When you clear out the mess, you not only find your old baseball cards but also create room for creativity and clarity. Who needs another pair of shoes when you can finally locate your remote control? By focusing on physical decluttering, you give your mind a chance to kick back, relax, and stop being overwhelmed by the chaos of the world. It's like giving your thoughts a spa day—complete with cucumber masks and calming music.

Now, let's talk about doomscrolling, that delightful pastime of scrolling through endless feeds of negativity and cat videos that somehow always leave you feeling like you just binge-watched a horror movie. If only scrolling could burn calories! Instead of letting algorithms dictate your mood, try decluttering your digital space. Unfollow that one friend who posts ten selfies a day and curate your feed to include more uplifting content. Replace doomscrolling with something productive—like scrolling through inspirational quotes. Suddenly, your mind is less of a dumpster fire and more like a cozy cabin in the woods, where you can sip tea and ponder life's mysteries without the weight of the world on your shoulders.

And speaking of weight, let's tackle the junk food conundrum. We all know the siren song of pizza rolls and nachos can be impossible to resist, especially after a long day of pretending to be an adult. But when your kitchen resembles a fast-food drive-thru, it's time for a culinary declutter. Start by clearing out expired snacks and replacing them with healthier options that won't make your body feel like it's auditioning for a role in a medical drama. Embrace colorful fruits and veggies, and suddenly, you're not just cleaning out your pantry; you're upgrading your life. Who knew that a simple carrot stick could become your new best friend?

On the productivity front, a messy workspace is like trying to write a novel in a tornado. If your desk is more of a no-fly zone than a work zone, it's time to channel your inner minimalist. Toss out old papers, empty coffee cups, and those mysterious items you can't even identify. A clean workspace can lead to a clear mind, allowing you to finally tackle that to-do list that has been staring at you like a disgruntled cat. Establish a daily routine that includes time for both work and play. You'll not only feel accomplished but might also discover that you're capable of adulting—who knew?

Finally, let's address the elephant in the room: anxiety. It's like that clingy friend who won't let you hang out with anyone else. Decluttering your mental space means learning to let go of things that don't serve you. Practice mindfulness and focus on the present instead of fretting about the past or future. As you clear out unnecessary thoughts, you'll make room for positivity and growth. Embrace the journey of building healthy habits, and you might just find that moving forward isn't so daunting after all. So grab a trash bag, a healthy snack, and a playlist of your favorite tunes, and let the decluttering begin!

Minimalism: Less is More

Imagine waking up one day and realizing your life feels like a cluttered attic where you can't find the box marked "joy" because it's buried under a mountain of stuff. Minimalism isn't just about having fewer things; it's about making space for what truly matters. If you've ever stared at your phone for hours, doomscrolling through an endless feed of cat videos and conspiracy theories, you might be due for a minimalism intervention. Spoiler alert: You don't need a degree in decluttering from the University of Overwhelming Stuff to start feeling lighter and more focused.

Let's talk about algorithms. You know, those sneaky little programs that think they know you better than your best friend. They'll keep feeding you the same negativity, junk food recipes, and self-help articles that make you feel worse instead of better. By practicing minimalism, you can take back control. Imagine curating your digital space the way you would your wardrobe. Get rid of the content that doesn't spark joy (or at least a mild sense of amusement) and make room for the things that lift you up. The less cluttered your mind, the fewer distractions you have when you're trying to focus on actually accomplishing your goals—like finding your keys or remembering to eat something that's not a donut.

Now, let's address that thing called the Standard American Diet. If your idea of a balanced meal is a pizza in one hand and a soda in the other, it's time to rethink your choices. Minimalism applies to your plate too. Imagine if you replaced the junk food with colorful, vibrant fruits and veggies. Not only would your meals be more Instagram-worthy, but you'd also start feeling like a superhero on a mission to conquer life—one healthy bite at a time. Plus, when you eat better, you'll find it easier to kick that inertia loop you've been stuck in, where moving from the couch to the fridge feels like running a marathon.

Feeling overwhelmed? Join the club. It's a membership that nobody signed up for but seems to have a never-ending waiting list. By adopting a minimalist approach to your daily routine, you can eliminate the chaos. Start each day with a few essential tasks that are manageable and meaningful, rather than a to-do list that could rival War and Peace. This way, you'll feel the sweet satisfaction of accomplishment and might just discover that the world doesn't end if you don't respond to every single email at 3 a.m.

Finally, let's not forget the importance of self-care and sleep hygiene in this minimalist journey. The less clutter you have in your life, both physically and mentally, the more energy you can devote to rest and relaxation. Create a peaceful nighttime routine that helps you unwind and recharge. No more scrolling through social media until your eyes bleed; instead, how about reading a book or meditating? Your future self will thank you, and you'll wake up feeling like a well-rested, decluttered version of yourself, ready to take on the day without that pesky stress weighing you down.

Chapter 8: Organizing for the Disorganized

Tools for Tackling Chaos

In a world overflowing with distractions, it's no wonder that chaos feels like your relentless best friend, always hanging around, ready to derail your best intentions. If you're scrolling through your phone while trying to figure out how to fit in exercise, eat right, and keep your room from resembling a post-apocalyptic movie set, you're not alone. The first tool in our chaos-fighting toolkit is digital wellness. Set boundaries with your screen time. Try a digital detox: put your phone in another room while you eat, or better yet, wear a blindfold if necessary. You'll be amazed at how much more you can accomplish when you're not being lured into the black hole of doomscrolling and algorithm-driven rabbit holes that make you question your existence.

Next up, let's talk about nutrition. The standard American diet, with its penchant for junk food, is like that friend who keeps dragging you into bad decisions. It's time to break up! Embrace the colorful world of fruits and vegetables. They're not just for Instagram photos; they actually make you feel good, unlike that third slice of pizza that seemed like a great idea at the time. Try meal prepping on a Sunday so you're not staring blankly at an empty fridge after a long day, contemplating whether cereal is a valid dinner option. Spoiler alert: it's not!

Now, for the busy bees who feel like they're perpetually stuck in the inertia loop, time management is your secret weapon. Get yourself a planner or download an app that doesn't suck the life out of you. Break your day into manageable chunks; tackle one task at a time. If you find yourself staring at a to-do list longer than a CVS receipt, just remember: Rome wasn't built in a day, and neither will your dream life be. Celebrate small wins! Did you finally fold that laundry? Bravo! Reward yourself with a dance party, not a Netflix binge.

Let's not forget about mental health; it's like the unsung hero of your chaos-fighting toolkit. Practicing mindfulness can be as simple as taking a few deep breaths or staring at a wall for five minutes and contemplating your life choices. If you're feeling overwhelmed, try journaling. Write down your thoughts, fears, and grocery lists. It's therapeutic and an excellent way to clear out the clutter in your mind. Plus, you'll finally remember to buy toilet paper.

Finally, embrace minimalism and decluttering. If your space looks like a hoarder's paradise, it's time for a clean-up. Start small— pick one drawer or corner and make it your mission to conquer it. Throw out what you don't need, and for goodness' sake, stop holding onto that broken lamp from college. Remember, a tidy space equals a tidy mind. As you tackle chaos, remember that progress is a journey. With the right tools, a sprinkle of humor, and a dash of determination, you can move forward and create a fulfilling life that even chaos would envy.

ADHD and Focus: Finding Your Flow

Ah, ADHD, the quirky brain wiring that turns focus into a game of hide-and-seek. For those of us navigating life with this delightful condition, achieving that elusive "flow" can feel like trying to find a unicorn in a haystack. The world is full of distractions, from social media rabbit holes to the siren song of junk food. Yet, fear not! With a sprinkle of humor and a dash of practical tips, we can tackle the chaos and learn how to turn our attention into a superpower instead of a super nuisance.

First things first, let's address the doomscrolling epidemic. You know the drill: one minute you're checking the weather, and the next, you're knee-deep in conspiracy theories about alien invasions. Instead of letting algorithms dictate your life, try setting a timer. Yes, I mean it! Give yourself a solid ten minutes to scroll through Instagram, and then boom—enforced break time. Go grab a snack that doesn't come from a neon bag and remind yourself that while the world is indeed on fire, your sanity is worth more than viral cat videos.

Now, let's talk about clutter, the silent partner in our ADHD journey. It's like a messy roommate you didn't invite in but who's now hogging your space. A chaotic environment can sabotage your focus faster than you can say "where's my other shoe?" Embrace minimalism, not as a trendy lifestyle choice, but as a survival strategy. Start small: tackle one area of your room or workspace at a time. You'd be amazed at how a clean desk can lead to a clean mind. Plus, you'll finally find that elusive pair of scissors you swore you lost to the Bermuda Triangle of clutter.

Next up, let's dive into the joys of time management. Picture this: instead of being a procrastination ninja, you become the master of your schedule. Use a planner or an app to block out your day, including breaks to recharge. And don't forget to schedule in some exercise because, believe it or not, moving your body can help you focus better. Even a quick dance party in your living room can get those dopamine levels rising and put you in the groove to tackle those pesky tasks. Just try not to scare the cat with your moves.

Finally, let's talk about sleep, the misunderstood hero of productivity. If you're feeling overwhelmed, stressed, or just plain lost, chances are your sleep hygiene is in the toilet. Set a bedtime, create a cozy sleep sanctuary, and ditch the screens an hour before you hit the hay. Your brain will thank you as it gears up for another day of navigating life with ADHD. Remember, finding your flow is not about perfection; it's about progress. So, embrace the chaos, laugh at the mishaps, and keep moving forward. After all, the best part of the journey is that ridiculous dance party you have along the way.

The Art of Prioritizing

Prioritizing is like playing a game of Tetris with your life, where the blocks are your tasks, and if you're not careful, they'll pile up until you're buried under a mountain of unfinished business. Imagine a typical day: you wake up, and immediately the digital world starts calling your name. Social media notifications, emails, and a plethora of streaming options bombard you, all begging for your attention. You could scroll through cat videos (which are undeniably adorable) or dive into an endless rabbit hole of conspiracy theories, but do you really want to sacrifice precious hours that could have been spent actually getting things done? Spoiler alert: the answer is no, unless you want to become the reigning champion of procrastination.

Now, let's talk about the infamous "to-do" list. You might think it's just a fancy way to throw your hopes and dreams onto a piece of paper, but let me tell you, it can be your best friend if you treat it right. Instead of listing everything like a grocery list for a junk food binge, try prioritizing tasks by urgency and importance. Start with the things that absolutely cannot wait, like turning in that project or, heaven forbid, paying your bills before the lights go out. Then, sprinkle in some smaller tasks—like cleaning your room or responding to that friend who keeps texting you about their new diet. Remember, a cluttered list leads to a cluttered mind, and if your mind's cluttered, good luck getting anything done without feeling overwhelmed.

But wait, there's more! The art of prioritizing isn't just about managing tasks; it's about managing your energy and mental health, too. Ever notice how binge-watching a show feels like a productive use of time until, suddenly, you realize it's 3 AM and you have to be up for work in three hours? Yeah, that's the dopamine monster at work, and it loves to keep you awake. Instead of letting your brain get hijacked by mindless scrolling or junk food runs, try to find activities that recharge you. Whether it's a brisk walk, a dance-off in your living room, or even reading a book that doesn't involve vampires or dystopian futures, making time for rejuvenation will keep you sharp when it's time to tackle that to-do list.

Speaking of rejuvenation, let's not forget the power of a solid routine. Creating a daily structure is like giving your life a GPS; it helps you navigate through the chaos. Start your day with a few small wins—make your bed, have a healthy breakfast, and set a clear intention for what you want to accomplish. These little victories can snowball into something much bigger and more meaningful. Plus, a routine can help you dodge the inertia loop that keeps you stuck in a cycle of doomscrolling and junk food binges. And hey, a little humor goes a long way. When you look at your daily tasks, try to find the hilarity in them. Why not laugh at the absurdity of adulting? It makes the grind a whole lot lighter.

Finally, remember that prioritizing is a skill, not a superpower. It's okay to stumble and trip over your own to-do list sometimes. Everyone has days when they feel like a disorganized mess, especially when life throws curveballs your way. Embrace the chaos, learn from it, and keep moving forward. The secret is to keep adjusting and refining your approach until you find what works for you. Prioritizing might not come naturally at first, but with practice, you'll find yourself climbing out of that pile of clutter and chaos, one task at a time, and maybe even cracking a smile while you do it. After all, life's too short to take it all too seriously!

Chapter 9: Anxiety and the Overwhelm Factor

Identifying Triggers: What Makes You Tick?

Identifying triggers is like playing detective in your own life, except you're not wearing a trench coat or carrying a magnifying glass. Instead, you might be found scrolling through your phone, munching on that suspiciously neon-colored snack, or contemplating the existential dread of your to-do list. So, what makes you tick? No, I'm not asking about your favorite TikTok dance or the latest Netflix binge—I'm talking about the sneaky little things that lead you down the rabbit hole of doomscrolling or the bottomless pit of junk food. Grab your magnifying glass, because it's time to examine the culprits behind your habits.

Imagine this: you're mindlessly scrolling through social media, and suddenly, you find yourself knee-deep in a conspiracy theory about how pigeons are government drones. That's a trigger, my friend! It could be boredom, loneliness, or perhaps the need for a little excitement in an otherwise mundane day. Recognizing these triggers is essential because they can lead you to develop habits that aren't exactly on the "healthy" side of life. Instead of becoming a professional pigeon theorist, you might consider redirecting that energy into a hobby, like doodling or even, gasp, reading a book!

Now, let's talk about food. You know that moment when you're stress-eating a bag of chips while contemplating your life choices? That's a classic trigger scenario. Stress, anxiety, and a lack of sleep can send you straight into the arms of the snack cupboard. To combat this, keep a journal of your eating habits and note when you reach for that bag of chips. Spoiler alert: it's usually when Netflix is at its most dramatic. By identifying these patterns, you can start swapping out those crunchy, salty snacks for something that doesn't make your body feel like a dumpster fire—like fruit or yogurt.

Now, let's not ignore the clutches of digital distractions. Algorithms are like that friend who just won't stop suggesting the same terrible movie. They'll keep feeding you content that keeps you glued to your screen, but not in a way that actually enriches your life—think more "How to Train Your Dragon" and less "How to Train Yourself." Recognizing when you're caught in an echo chamber can help you break free. Set a timer for your social media usage, and when it goes off, do something that doesn't involve staring at a screen. Maybe go for a walk, or better yet, go outside and stare at actual clouds instead of your feed.

In the grand circus of life, identifying your triggers is the first step in taking control of your habits. Whether you're feeling overwhelmed, disorganized, or just plain lost, remember that you have the power to change your narrative. It's about understanding what makes you tick and choosing to respond with intention rather than inertia. So, grab that journal, note those triggers, and get ready to rewrite the script of your life. It's time to move forward, one habit at a time, preferably without the pigeons!

Breathing Techniques for Instant Calm

Breathing techniques can be the secret weapon in your arsenal against the chaos of modern life, and trust me, we all need a little more calm in our lives. Imagine this: you're knee-deep in doomscrolling, your thumb is getting a workout that would make a personal trainer weep, and your mind is racing faster than a squirrel on an espresso binge. Just when you think you're about to lose it, all you have to do is take a moment and breathe. Yes, breathe! It sounds simple, but it's like hitting the reset button on your brain. So, let's dive into some breathing techniques that could transform you from a stress monster into a zen master faster than you can say "I need a snack."

First up is the classic deep belly breathing. This isn't just for yoga enthusiasts; it's for anyone who has ever felt overwhelmed, which is basically all of us. Picture yourself lying on the floor like a starfish, or sitting in your favorite chair. Close your eyes and inhale deeply through your nose, letting your belly expand like a balloon. Then exhale slowly through your mouth like you're blowing out birthday candles. Do this a few times and suddenly, that mountain of laundry or the endless to-do list doesn't seem so terrifying. In fact, it might even look manageable, or at least less like a scene from a horror movie.

Next, let's talk about the 4-7-8 technique. This one sounds fancy, but it's as easy as pie—just without the calories. Breathe in for a count of four, hold for a count of seven, and then exhale for a count of eight. Repeat this cycle a few times, and you'll feel like you've just stepped out of a spa, even if you're sitting on a pile of dirty clothes. It's like giving your brain a mini vacation while the rest of the world keeps spinning. Plus, it's a great way to keep that inner critic quiet, which will thank you later when you decide to tackle your cluttered room instead of scrolling through social media.

Let's not forget about box breathing, a technique used by everyone from athletes to Navy SEALs. You breathe in for four counts, hold for four counts, exhale for four counts, and hold again for four counts. It's a cycle that resembles a box, hence the name. It's perfect for anyone feeling like they've been stuck in a never-ending loop of procrastination and anxiety. Visualizing your breath as a box can also help you keep your thoughts contained, preventing them from spilling out like a bag of chips you accidentally dropped on the floor.

Lastly, let's incorporate some laughter into our breathing routine. Yes, you heard me right. Laughter is like a breath of fresh air, and it releases all those feel-good chemicals in your brain faster than you can say "I can't believe I procrastinated for three hours." Try the "laughing breath" technique—take a deep breath in, and as you exhale, let out a laugh. It may feel silly at first, but who doesn't need a good chuckle when life gets too serious? Plus, it's a fantastic way to engage your friends or family and turn a moment of stress into a mini comedy show.

In conclusion, mastering these breathing techniques can be your ticket to instant calm in the whirlwind of life. Whether you're a busy young adult drowning in responsibilities or a senior feeling a bit lost in this fast-paced world, taking a moment to breathe can help you reset your mind and reclaim your focus. So the next time you feel overwhelmed, remember: breathe, laugh, and tackle those tasks with a newfound sense of calm. Who knew that such a simple act could be the gateway to a healthier, happier you?

Building Emotional Resilience

Emotional resilience is like that secret superhero cape you didn't know you had until you stumbled through a series of unfortunate events, like a series of bad Netflix recommendations or accidentally liking a five-year-old post from your crush. It's the ability to bounce back from life's curveballs, whether that's a bad breakup, a missed deadline, or realizing that you've eaten an entire box of cookies while watching reality TV. To build this resilience, the first step is to recognize that life can be messy, and that's perfectly okay. Embrace the chaos! Accept that sometimes you'll doomscroll for hours, but hey, awareness is half the battle, right?

Next up, let's tackle the algorithms that seem to know us better than our best friends. If you're constantly bombarded with videos of cute cats and conspiracy theories, it's time for a digital detox. Try replacing that mindless scrolling with something that actually feeds your brain, like reading a book or attempting to cook a meal that doesn't involve a microwave. Remember to seek out diverse perspectives; it's like adding different toppings to your pizza. You wouldn't want to eat plain cheese every day, would you? Balance in your online consumption can prevent you from getting trapped in an echo chamber of negativity and junk food for thought.

Now let's address the elephant in the room: clutter. Clutter isn't just physical; it's also mental. Ever try to focus on a task while your desk resembles a post-apocalyptic battlefield? Cleaning up that mess can do wonders for your mental clarity. Start small; tackle one drawer or corner at a time. You'll be amazed at how a little decluttering not only clears your space but also clears your mind. Plus, you'll find things you thought were lost forever, like your favorite pen or that one sock that never found its match.

Speaking of clarity, let's chat about routines. Creating a daily routine doesn't have to feel like waking up for a 6 AM boot camp. Start with simple goals, like drinking a glass of water first thing in the morning, or taking a five-minute stretch break. Gradually build that into a routine that works for you, and you may find that you're less anxious and more productive. Who knew that establishing a rhythm could help you feel less like a chaotic tornado and more like a well-oiled machine? Trust me, it's much easier to tackle your goals when you're not dodging debris from yesterday's emotional hurricane.

Finally, remember that emotional resilience isn't about being unshakeable; it's about knowing how to pick yourself up after the inevitable spills and crashes. Life will throw junk food, poor sleep, and stress your way, but with the right mindset and a sprinkle of humor, you can navigate through it. So, next time you feel overwhelmed, take a breath, laugh at the absurdity of it all, and remind yourself that you're a work in progress. After all, even superheroes had to start somewhere before they donned that cape!

Chapter 10: The Dopamine Dilemma

Understanding Dopamine: The Good, The Bad, The Addictive

Dopamine is often hailed as the "feel-good" neurotransmitter, but let's be real: it can also be a sneaky little rascal that gets us into all sorts of trouble. Imagine dopamine as that friend who always convinces you to binge-watch another episode of your favorite show instead of doing your homework. Sure, that quick dopamine hit from a dramatic cliffhanger feels fantastic, but before you know it, it's 3 a.m., and you're questioning your life choices while surrounded by empty snack bags. Understanding dopamine is crucial because it influences everything from our eating habits to our productivity levels, and let's face it, nobody wants to be the person who talks about how great they are at procrastination.

Now, let's talk about the dark side of dopamine. It's like that classic horror movie twist where you think everything is fine, and then—bam!—you realize that endless scrolling through social media is more addictive than that last slice of pizza you promised yourself you wouldn't eat. Algorithms are designed to keep you hooked, feeding you content that aligns with your interests and keeps you in a cozy echo chamber. It's like being in a relationship with someone who only tells you what you want to hear, making it way too easy to ignore the fact that you're neglecting your responsibilities—like cleaning your room or getting that elusive workout in. Spoiler alert: it's not a healthy relationship.

But wait, there's more! Dopamine can also lead to some seriously chaotic behavior, like diving headfirst into the world of junk food. Ever found yourself knee-deep in a tub of ice cream after a tough day? That dopamine rush feels amazing until you're left feeling sluggish and regretting your life choices. The Standard American

Diet might be a delicious way to indulge your cravings, but it's more like a roller coaster ride—highs followed by some serious lows. You're left battling anxiety and feeling overwhelmed, which only makes you crave more of that sweet, sweet dopamine to lift your spirits. It's a vicious cycle that nobody signed up for.

Now, don't throw in the towel just yet! Understanding how to build a healthier relationship with dopamine can help you reclaim your life from the clutches of chaos. Picture this: instead of mindlessly scrolling through your phone, you could channel that energy into establishing a daily routine that actually makes you feel accomplished. Imagine waking up, going for a run, and eating a nutritious breakfast, all while feeling like an absolute rock star. Your brain will start to associate those positive habits with dopamine hits, leading you to feel more motivated and less like a disorganized mess. Trust us, your future self will thank you for it.

Finally, let's not forget the importance of balance. Dopamine isn't the enemy; it's all about how you use it. Think of it as a mischievous little buddy who needs some guidance. By incorporating mindfulness, healthy eating, and a sprinkle of organization into your life, you can create a harmonious relationship with dopamine. So whether you're a busy professional, a student drowning in assignments, or a senior trying to figure out what's next, embracing the good, the bad, and the addictive nature of dopamine can lead to a fulfilling life. Just remember, every time you resist the urge to scroll, you're one step closer to moving forward and becoming the best version of yourself.

Finding Balance in a Pleasure-Driven World

In a world where scrolling through social media can feel like a competitive sport, finding balance is akin to trying to juggle flaming torches while riding a unicycle. Seriously, how did we end up here? One moment you're checking the weather, and the next, you're knee-deep in videos of cats playing pianos. It's a digital rabbit hole that can lead to doomscrolling—where we consume endless streams of negativity and chaos. The algorithms have become our modern-day puppeteers, pulling our strings and keeping us glued to screens. So, how do we escape this digital circus and regain control over our time and attention?

First things first, let's tackle the elephant in the room: junk food. You might think that a bag of chips is the perfect sidekick while you binge-watch your favorite series, but it's like inviting a raccoon into your kitchen. One snack leads to another, and before you know it, you've consumed an entire pizza while half-heartedly paying attention to a show about extreme couponing. Instead of giving in to the allure of the Standard American Diet, let's spice things up with some nutritious alternatives. Think of it as upgrading from a floppy disk to a high-speed SSD—your body and mind will thank you for the boost!

Now that we've addressed our snack habits, let's talk about routines—specifically, the ones we don't have. If your daily life feels like a never-ending game of Tetris with tasks piling up and no clear strategy, it's time to hit the pause button. Creating a routine doesn't mean you have to become a robot; it's more like finding a rhythm that works for you. Start small—like setting a timer for 10 minutes to tidy your room. You'll be amazed at how much better you feel when you can see your floor again. Plus, a little organization can do wonders for your mental clarity, helping you dodge that nasty inertia loop.

Speaking of mental clarity, let's chat about sleep. Are you one of those people who think sleep is for the weak? Newsflash: sleep deprivation is the ultimate villain in your quest for balance. It's like trying to run a marathon on empty; you'll trip over your own shoelaces. Prioritizing sleep hygiene can be a game-changer. Create a cozy bedtime routine that doesn't involve scrolling through your phone until your eyes bleed. Instead, consider indulging in a good book or practicing mindfulness. Your brain will thank you, and you might just wake up feeling like a superhero ready to conquer the day.

Finally, let's address the clutter in your life—both physical and mental. If your desk looks like a tornado hit it and your mind is a chaotic mess of "What do I do next?" you're not alone. Embrace minimalism like it's the latest trend. Start by decluttering one small area at a time. Trust me, tossing out that old pizza box from last month will feel like a victory. As you create space in your environment, you'll create space in your mind too. Balance in a pleasure-driven world isn't about denying yourself joy; it's about making conscious choices that lead to a fulfilling life. So, take a deep breath, put down the chips, and let's move forward together!

Healthy Alternatives to Instant Gratification

Finding healthy alternatives to instant gratification can feel like trying to find a unicorn in a haystack. We live in a world that screams convenience and instant results, from binge-watching shows to scrolling through social media like it's an Olympic sport. But let's face it, those quick fixes often leave us feeling emptier than a bag of chips after a Netflix marathon. Instead of falling for the allure of instant satisfaction, let's explore some alternatives that not only fill your time but also add some pizzazz to your life.

First up, let's tackle the doomscrolling dilemma. Instead of diving headfirst into the latest negative news, how about immersing yourself in a book? Yes, those things with pages! Reading can expand your mind and allow you to escape into different worlds. Plus, it has the added benefit of making you look smart at parties. If you're feeling particularly adventurous, try picking up a hobby. Knitting, painting, or even learning to juggle can be a great way to channel that desire for instant fun into something that's actually fulfilling. Who knows, you might just discover a hidden talent that wins you a spot on a reality show!

Next on our list is the temptation of junk food. We've all been there: a long day, a tub of ice cream calling your name, and suddenly, you're two seasons deep into a show with a spoon in hand. Instead, let's consider the wonders of meal prepping. It might sound as exciting as watching paint dry, but preparing healthy meals in advance can save you from those late-night snack attacks. Plus, when you finally sink your teeth into that colorful salad you prepped, you'll feel like the culinary king or queen you were always meant to be. Say goodbye to the standard American diet and hello to a plate that's as vibrant as your future!

Now, let's address the clutter in our lives—both physical and mental. If your room looks like a tornado hit it, it's no wonder you're feeling overwhelmed. Start small by decluttering one corner of your space. You'd be amazed at how much clearer your mind becomes when there's a little less chaos around you. And while you're at it, consider setting up a daily routine. Yes, I know it sounds as thrilling as watching grass grow, but routines can be your best friends in the battle against inertia. They provide structure, help you tackle important tasks, and can even make you feel like a grown-up—minus the adulting anxiety that often accompanies it.

Lastly, let's chat about sleep hygiene. If you're scrolling through your phone at 3 AM, you're not winning any awards for restfulness. Instead, try creating a bedtime routine that would make a sleep expert proud. Ditch the screens an hour before bed, read a book, or try some meditation. Your future self will thank you when you wake up feeling like a million bucks instead of a zombie who just survived a horror movie. Remember, healthy alternatives to instant gratification require a little effort, but the rewards are worth it. Embrace the journey of building healthy habits, and you'll find that the fulfillment you seek is just a few steps away!

Chapter 11: Sleep: Your Best Friend or Worst Enemy?

Why Sleep Hygiene Matters

Sleep hygiene is not just a fancy term to make you feel guilty about binge-watching your favorite series until the wee hours of the morning. It's the secret sauce that can transform your life from a chaotic whirlwind of half-finished tasks and missed deadlines into a smooth, productive ride on the express train to Awesometown. Picture this: you wake up after a solid night of sleep, feeling like a superstar ready to conquer the world, instead of a zombie who's one cup of coffee away from a complete meltdown. Good sleep hygiene can help you escape the doomscrolling trap and put an end to those late-night snack raids on the fridge that leave you feeling more like a junk food junkie than a health-conscious adult.

Establishing a solid sleep routine is like creating a superhero cape for your mental health. When you prioritize sleep, you help your brain combat negativity and anxiety, which often feel like that annoying friend who just won't leave the party. Instead of spiraling down an echo chamber of doom and gloom, a good night's sleep can boost your mood and help you tackle the day with a positive mindset. So, why not trade in those late-night TikTok marathons for a cozy bedtime routine that involves a book, some herbal tea, and maybe a gentle stretch? Your future self will thank you, and you might just wake up with the energy to declutter that messy room or tackle that to-do list that seems to grow by the minute.

Now, let's talk about the relationship between sleep and productivity. If you're feeling overwhelmed and constantly busy without actually accomplishing anything, it's probably time to examine your sleep habits. When you skimp on sleep, it's like driving a car on fumes—eventually, you're going to stall. A well-rested brain is sharper, more focused, and ready to crush those goals instead of letting them gather dust in the corner. Embracing proper sleep hygiene can help you manage your time better, allowing you to create a daily routine that doesn't feel like you're running a marathon every day. Who knew that hitting the sack could actually help you run faster toward your dreams?

Sleep hygiene also plays a critical role in your physical health. If you're stuck in the cycle of poor eating habits and late-night junk food runs, it's time to break free. Adequate sleep helps regulate your appetite and can even curb those cravings for unhealthy snacks that seem to whisper sweet nothings to you at midnight. When you sleep well, you're more likely to make healthier choices throughout the day, which is a win-win. You'll have more energy to move your body and maybe even take up a fun new exercise routine instead of scrolling through social media while contemplating your life choices at 3 a.m.

In a world where distractions are just a click away, prioritizing sleep hygiene is your ticket to reclaiming control over your life. It's not just about shutting your eyes for a few hours; it's about creating an environment and routine that supports your overall well-being. So, turn off those notifications, make your bedroom a sleep sanctuary, and say goodbye to the disorganization of your sleep life. By putting sleep hygiene into action, you'll not only feel better but also become the best version of yourself. And who doesn't want to wake up ready to take on the world instead of wrestling with the blankets like a contestant on a reality show?

Tips for a Restful Night's Sleep

Sleep is not just a luxury; it's an essential part of life that gets overlooked in the whirlwind of our busy schedules. Picture this: you're scrolling through your phone at 2 a.m., convinced that the latest meme about cats will somehow solve all your problems. Spoiler alert: it won't. Instead, it's time to kick that doomscrolling habit to the curb and embrace some good ol' sleep hygiene. Start by creating a bedtime routine that would make even the sleepiest sloth jealous. Dim the lights, put your phone in a different room (yes, it can survive without you for eight hours), and try reading a book or sipping some herbal tea. Your future self will thank you for not turning into a zombie by morning.

Now, let's talk about your bedroom. If it looks like a tornado passed through, chances are your sleep quality is about as good as a soggy pizza. Clutter can create a chaotic environment that makes it hard to relax. So, channel your inner Marie Kondo and declutter your space. Toss out the junk, put everything in its place, and create a sleep sanctuary that radiates calm vibes. Remember, a tidy space equals a tidy mind, or at least a mind that's not spiraling into the abyss of "What did I forget to do today?"

Nutrition also plays a role in your beauty sleep. If you're bingeing on junk food while watching Netflix, your body might be throwing a mini revolt. Instead of reaching for that bag of chips, consider a light snack that won't send your body into a sugar-fueled frenzy. Think yogurt, fruit, or nuts—snacks that say, "I care about my health and my sleep." Plus, being mindful about what you eat can help you avoid those post-midnight regrets that keep you tossing and turning all night long.

Exercise might sound like a word that's been thrown around more than your favorite party game, but it can actually help you sleep better. Even a brisk walk can be a lifesaver for your sleep cycle. It's like giving your body a little nudge to remind it that it's time to wind down. Plus, who doesn't want to feel a little more accomplished? Getting your body moving during the day can help you feel less like a couch potato and more like an actual functioning adult. And hey, if you can sneak in some time for exercise while binge-watching your favorite show, even better!

Finally, let's talk about mental health. Your brain is like a smartphone that's been running too many apps at once— overheated and ready to crash. Practice mindfulness techniques, like meditation or deep breathing, to help calm that chaotic mind of yours. When you let go of the stress and anxiety that weighs you down, you'll find it easier to slide into those sweet dreams. So, take a deep breath, let the worries of the day drift away, and remember: a good night's sleep is just a few mindful habits away. Embrace these tips, and you might just wake up feeling like a superhero ready to take on the world.

Napping: A Lost Art

Ah, the nap — that glorious slice of heaven that seems to have vanished from our busy lives. For teenagers and young adults, the thought of napping might evoke images of lazy afternoons spent on a couch, which is basically a crime against productivity. But let's be real: if you've ever spent hours doomscrolling through social media or binging an entire season of a show, you know that naps are the ultimate act of rebellion against the tyranny of that never-ending to-do list. Imagine trading those mindless scrolling sessions for a power nap that leaves you refreshed and ready to conquer the world (or at least tackle your laundry).

For busy working people or anyone juggling a million tasks, napping is often seen as a luxury, reserved for toddlers or retired folks who have already conquered life. But here's the kicker: a quick snooze can actually boost your productivity and creativity. It's like hitting the reset button on your brain. Instead of reaching for yet another cup of coffee (which, let's face it, is just a fancy way of saying you're trying to caffeinate your way through anxiety), consider sneaking in a 20-minute nap. Your brain will thank you, and you might find yourself not just functioning, but thriving. Who knew that the secret to adulting could be as simple as shutting your eyes for a few minutes?

Now, let's address the elephant in the room: our obsession with technology and the glorification of being busy. We've fallen into an inertia loop, where we feel guilty for taking a break. Napping has become synonymous with laziness, and that's just plain wrong. Our ancestors napped like pros, and they didn't have TikTok to distract them. If you're feeling overwhelmed by clutter, disorganization, and the pressures of life, a little nap can provide the mental clarity needed to tackle those messes. It's like giving your brain a quick spa day. Plus, it's an excellent excuse to escape from the chaos for a bit.

For those grappling with anxiety or ADHD, naps can be a game changer. They help reset your focus and calm your racing thoughts. Think of it as a mini-vacation for your mind. Sure, you could spend that time stressing over your unmade bed or the pile of dishes in the sink, but why not embrace the art of napping instead? Set a timer, cozy up, and let yourself drift off. When you wake up, you might just find that the clutter isn't as daunting as it seemed, and you're ready to tackle those important tasks with renewed vigor.

In a world that often glorifies busyness and productivity, it's time to reclaim the lost art of napping. It's not just about catching some

Z's; it's about taking a stand against the chaos of modern life. So, the next time you catch yourself scrolling through endless cat videos or letting anxiety spiral, remember that a well-timed nap could be your secret weapon. Embrace it, and you might just find that moving forward in life becomes a whole lot easier — and way more fun.

Chapter 12: Stress Management 101

Recognizing Stress Before It Recognizes You

Recognizing stress before it recognizes you is like spotting a cockroach in your kitchen—it's much easier to deal with before it throws a rave party. Stress sneaks up on you, often disguised as a busy schedule, a pile of laundry that could double as a mountain range, or that dreaded notification from your phone reminding you of yet another deadline. To tackle this sneaky little gremlin, you first need to become the Sherlock Holmes of your own life. Learn to observe those telltale signs: the tightening in your chest when you open your email, the way your brain feels like a blender set to "puree" when you think about your to-do list, and the existential crisis you have every time you scroll through social media and compare your life to perfectly curated influencer feeds.

Most of us have fallen victim to the charming allure of doomscrolling, where one minute you're checking the news, and the next you're deep-diving into videos of cats playing piano. It's a slippery slope that often leads to a digital rabbit hole filled with negativity and anxiety. Instead of feeding the algorithm that thrives on chaos, try to limit your screen time and replace it with activities that boost your mood. Remember, the last thing you need is to spiral into an echo chamber where everyone is as stressed out as you are. Take a break and watch something that makes you laugh, like a classic sitcom or a documentary about the world's funniest animals—trust me, they're out there.

Now, let's talk about nutrition because we all know that a bag of chips may feel like a warm hug in the moment but will leave you feeling like a potato later. Eating junk food is a quick fix for stress but ultimately a recipe for disaster. Think of your body as a high-performance vehicle; you wouldn't fill it with low-grade gasoline, right? So, swap those chips for some colorful veggies and fruits that make you feel like the superhero you truly are. If cooking feels like an Olympic sport, try simple recipes that are quicker than your favorite TikTok dance. Your brain will thank you, and your body will stop staging protests during important Zoom calls.

Next on the agenda is decluttering your life. No one can thrive in a space that looks like a tornado hit it—unless, of course, you're a contestant on a hoarding reality show. Start small: tackle one corner of your room or that one pile of laundry that's become a permanent resident. Create a daily routine that incorporates tidying up, even if it's just for five minutes. You'll be amazed at how decluttering can clear not just your physical space but also your mental space. A clean room can lead to a clean mind, setting the stage for focus and productivity. Plus, you'll finally find that missing sock you've been searching for since last summer!

Finally, let's tackle the big "S" word: sleep. We live in a world that glorifies being busy, but let's be real—being a zombie is not a good look. Sleep deprivation is like trying to run a marathon in flip-flops; it just doesn't work. Prioritize sleep hygiene by creating a calming bedtime routine that doesn't involve the glow of your phone screen. Instead, consider reading a book, journaling, or meditating. You'll wake up feeling like a new person, ready to take on the world. Remember, stress is like that annoying party guest who won't leave; the best way to get rid of it is to make your environment as welcoming and restful as possible. Embrace these strategies, and you'll be the one in control, moving forward toward a healthier, happier life.

Techniques for Stress Reduction

Stress is like that uninvited guest at a party who just doesn't know when to leave. Whether you're a teenager juggling school and social life, a young adult navigating the chaos of work and relationships, or a busy professional drowning in emails, everyone faces stress. The first step to kicking this unwanted guest to the curb is to establish healthy habits that promote relaxation. Start by ditching the doomscrolling; those endless feeds of bad news are like eating a whole bag of chips—you know it's unhealthy, but it's just too tempting. Instead, set a timer for your social media usage and fill your time with activities that actually make you happy, like reading a book, going for a walk, or even experimenting with a new recipe that doesn't involve a microwave.

Next up is something we all love to do but often forget—breathe. Yes, that's right! Breathing is free and doesn't require a subscription. Practicing mindfulness and deep breathing exercises can help you hit the brakes on stress. Try taking five minutes a day to sit quietly, close your eyes, and inhale deeply. Focus on your breath as if it's the last slice of pizza at a party. Inhale the good vibes, exhale the negativity. If you find your mind wandering (which it will, because, hey, you have a million things on your plate), gently guide it back. It's like training a puppy; you wouldn't yell at it for not sitting right away, would you? So give yourself a break and just breathe.

Now, let's talk about clutter. Your space reflects your mental state, and if your room looks like a tornado just hit it, your mind might be feeling a little stormy as well. Embrace minimalism, even if you're not ready to get rid of your entire collection of vintage concert T-shirts. Start small—pick one area to declutter each week. You might find that your old high school notes from that class you definitely didn't need to take are taking up valuable space. A clean space can lead to a clear mind, making it easier to focus on your goals. Plus, you'll finally be able to find that pair of socks you swore you had!

Exercise doesn't have to be a chore; it can be a fun escape from stress. Whether it's a dance party in your living room or a short jog around the block, find ways to get your body moving. Remember, you don't have to run a marathon; even a brisk walk counts! Grab a friend and turn it into a social event. Chat about life, laugh at your mutual struggles, and before you know it, you'll forget you're even working out. It's all about mixing things up and making it enjoyable. No one ever said you have to be a fitness guru to get those endorphins flowing.

Lastly, prioritize sleep like it's your new favorite hobby. Sleep deprivation is like a sneaky thief that robs you of your energy and focus, leaving you a disheveled mess. Establish a sleep routine that would make even the most disciplined of seniors proud. Create a calming bedtime ritual, banish screens an hour before bed, and consider reading a book instead (preferably one that doesn't involve doomscrolling). Treat your sleep like a sacred appointment that you can't afford to miss. When you wake up refreshed, you'll tackle your day like a superhero ready to conquer any villain (or pile of laundry) that comes your way. Embrace these stress-reduction techniques, and you'll be well on your way to moving forward in life, one deep breath and decluttered space at a time.

Making Time for Self-Care

In the chaotic symphony of life—where we juggle work, school, social media, and that ever-present fridge full of leftover pizza—finding time for self-care can feel like trying to find a unicorn in a haystack. First things first: let's clarify what self-care really means. It's not just about taking bubble baths or binge-watching your favorite show (although those can be part of it). Self-care is about prioritizing your needs, whether mental, physical, or emotional, and actually putting them on your to-do list. Yes, you heard that right! Treat it like an appointment, because if you don't, those self-care sessions will probably be overshadowed by doomscrolling or scrolling through TikTok for six hours while your laundry piles up.

Now, let's talk about the elephant in the room: procrastination. We all have our reasons for dodging self-care like it's a final exam. Maybe you're convinced that scrolling through social media is more important than, say, eating a vegetable. Or perhaps you're paralyzed by the sheer number of choices—do I meditate, go for a walk, or just stare blankly at the wall? Here's the kicker: self-care doesn't have to be complicated. Start small. Set a timer for five minutes to breathe deeply, or make a deal with yourself to eat one piece of fruit today. The important part is to actually do it. And if you happen to eat that fruit while watching Netflix, well, that's multitasking, right?

For those of you feeling lost amid a sea of clutter—literal and metaphorical—let's focus on decluttering your life. You might think your mess is a reflection of your chaotic mind, but let's face it: it's also a great excuse to avoid doing something productive. Grab a trash bag and channel your inner Marie Kondo. If it doesn't spark joy (or at least serve a purpose), toss it. Your space will start to feel lighter, and who knows? You might even find that long-lost sock you thought was part of a conspiracy against you. Plus, a tidy environment can boost your mood and give you that extra push to tackle those pesky tasks you've been dodging.

Ah, sleep hygiene—the adulting skill nobody warned you about. If you're running on caffeine and sheer willpower, it's time to reassess your relationship with your pillow. A solid night's sleep can work wonders for your mental clarity and emotional resilience. Set a bedtime routine that doesn't involve scrolling through social media like it's a life-or-death situation. Try reading a book, stretching, or even practicing mindfulness. The goal here is to create a sanctuary for sleep that's free from distractions. Trust me, your future self will thank you when you wake up less like a zombie and more like a functioning human being.

Finally, let's talk about building positive habits. They're like your favorite pair of sneakers: comfortable, familiar, and way better than running around barefoot. Start by establishing a daily routine that includes a mix of work and play. Whether you're a busy student, a young professional, or a retiree wondering what to do with your time, design your day like a playlist. Include some self-care tracks to keep the vibe flowing. Remember, life is too short to spend it feeling overwhelmed. Embrace the chaos, sprinkle in some laughter, and make time for self-care—it's the best investment you'll ever make in yourself.

Chapter 13: Eating Well Without Losing Your Mind

Quick and Healthy Meal Prep

In a world where scrolling through your phone can feel like a full-time job, it's time to shift gears and invest those precious minutes into something more productive—like meal prep. Yes, you heard me right! Picture this: instead of mindlessly watching videos of cats playing piano or the latest TikTok dance challenge, you could be chopping veggies, sautéing chicken, and feeling like a culinary wizard. Meal prepping is not just a way to eat healthier; it's about reclaiming your time and sanity. Trust me, your future self will thank you when you're not staring blankly at the fridge at 8 PM wondering if pizza counts as a vegetable.

Now, before you roll your eyes and think, "I don't have time for that," let's break it down. Meal prep doesn't mean you have to channel your inner Gordon Ramsay and whip up a five-course meal every Sunday. Oh no, my friend! It can be as simple as making a big batch of quinoa, roasting a tray of mixed vegetables, and grilling a few chicken breasts. In less than an hour, you can have enough food to last you for days. Think of it like creating your own personal buffet that takes zero effort to serve. And if you fancy yourself a culinary artist, feel free to get creative with spices and sauces—just keep the fire extinguisher handy!

Feeling overwhelmed by the thought of planning meals? Fear not! Start small. Pick two or three recipes that you actually enjoy eating. You know, the ones that make your taste buds do a happy dance. Write down the ingredients, make a shopping list, and head to the grocery store like a boss. You'll be in and out faster than you can say "healthy lifestyle." Plus, think of all the time you'll save during the week when you can simply reach into your fridge instead of wrestling with takeout menus or the dreaded "What's for dinner?" existential crisis.

Let's talk about variety because nobody wants to eat the same sad meal every day. A little secret? Batch cooking allows you to mix and match! Cook a big pot of chili, roast some sweet potatoes, and grill a couple of salmon fillets. You can combine them in countless ways throughout the week. Chili over sweet potatoes? Yes, please! Salmon salad for lunch? Count me in! It's like a delicious game of Tetris, where the only goal is to make your taste buds happy while keeping the junk food at bay.

Finally, the cherry on top of this nutritious sundae: meal prepping helps you dodge the doomscrolling pitfall. Instead of getting sucked into a vortex of negativity or watching an endless loop of "10 things you didn't know about cats," you'll be focused on something tangible and rewarding. Plus, you'll be too busy enjoying your meal to care about the latest social media drama. So grab those containers, channel your inner chef, and take a step toward a healthier, more organized life. Your future self will not only thank you but might even throw a party in your honor—complete with healthy snacks, of course!

Snacks That Won't Sabotage You

Snacks can be the sneaky little gremlins that sabotage your healthy intentions faster than you can say "potato chip." You know the ones—those innocent-looking bags of crunchy bliss that whisper sweet nothings to you while you doomscroll through your phone. But fear not! We're diving into the world of snacks that won't lead you down the dark path of junk food despair. Instead of letting those sugary sirens take the wheel, let's explore some options that will keep your energy up and your mood intact, all while keeping your sanity in check.

First up, we have the classic popcorn—yes, the air-popped kind, not the cinema-sized butter bomb that has more calories than a meal itself. Popcorn is a whole grain, and it's as light as a feather, making it a perfect snack for those late-night Netflix binges that inevitably turn into a full-blown marathon. Sprinkle some nutritional yeast on it, and you've got a cheesy flavor without the guilt. You'll be munching away like a happy little squirrel, knowing you're fueling your body instead of putting it in a food coma.

Next, let's talk about the underestimated power of fruits and veggies. Sure, they might not have the allure of a chocolate bar, but hear me out! Carrot sticks and apple slices can be dipped in hummus or nut butter to elevate them from "meh" to "heck yes!" Plus, they're colorful, which makes your snack bowl look like a party. And if you're feeling especially rebellious, throw in some dark chocolate-covered almonds. They're like the grown-up version of candy, giving you that sweet satisfaction without sending your blood sugar on a rollercoaster ride.

Now, for those who find themselves perpetually stressed (and let's be real, who isn't?), consider a handful of nuts as your go-to snack. Almonds, walnuts, or pistachios are not only crunchy and satisfying but also packed with healthy fats that your brain will thank you for. Just be careful with portion sizes—it's easy to treat them like popcorn and suddenly find yourself at the bottom of the bag, wondering where it all went. Remember, moderation is key, unless you're discussing your favorite TV series plot twists, in which case, go all in!

If you're still feeling lost in the snack abyss, consider making your own energy balls. These little nuggets of joy are like the ultimate

DIY project that doesn't require a degree in craft-making. Combine oats, nut butter, honey, and maybe a few chocolate chips for good measure. Roll them into bite-sized balls and store them in the fridge. When life gets overwhelming, just grab one or two. It's a snack that says, "I've got my life together," even if the laundry is still piled up and the dishes are threatening a coup.

In conclusion, snacks don't have to be the enemy in your quest for a fulfilling life. With a little creativity and a touch of humor, you can enjoy tasty treats that nurture your body and keep you from feeling like you're spiraling into the depths of junk food despair. So next time you reach for that bag of chips, remember these alternatives and give your snack game a healthy upgrade. After all, you deserve snacks that support your journey, not sabotage it!

Enjoying Food Without Guilt

Eating should be a delightful experience, not a source of stress or guilt. Yet, here we are, faced with endless options of kale chips versus potato chips, and it feels like we're stuck in an episode of a cooking show gone wrong. For many, food is often more about what we shouldn't be eating rather than what we can enjoy. Instead of being a joy, eating can become a battle of willpower, with guilt lurking in the shadows, ready to pounce the moment we indulge in that slice of chocolate cake or the extra helping of fries. But guess what? It's time to kick that guilt to the curb and embrace a healthier relationship with food—one that involves laughter, joy, and maybe a little bit of cake.

Let's face it: we live in a world where algorithms dictate our snack choices and social media feeds overflow with images of perfectly plated avocado toast. It's easy to get caught up in the spiral of comparison, leading us to believe that unless we're eating quinoa salad every day, we're failing at life. Newsflash: we're not all influencers with perfectly curated meals and endless time on our hands. A pinch of a cheesy nacho or a scoop of ice cream doesn't make you a bad person; it just makes you human. The trick is to find a balance that allows you to enjoy those guilty pleasures without spiraling into an emotional black hole.

Mindful eating can help turn the tide from guilt-ridden munching to a more pleasurable experience. This means slowing down, putting your phone away, and actually tasting what you're eating. Sounds revolutionary, right? When you savor each bite, you're less likely to overindulge, and you'll actually appreciate your food. Plus, if you're really paying attention, that kale salad might just start to taste better than those greasy fries—okay, maybe not, but you get the point. The goal is to cultivate a mindset where food is fuel for your body and soul, but also an opportunity for joy and connection.

Let's not forget the power of moderation. Rather than going on a fad diet that feels more like a punishment than a lifestyle, why not adopt a more flexible approach? Allow yourself to enjoy a variety of foods without labeling them as "good" or "bad." It's like a buffet of life—grab a little bit of everything! This can help reduce the urge to binge when you finally allow yourself a treat. Remember, it's not about the occasional indulgence; it's about how we approach food day in and day out. So, next time you find yourself reaching for that donut, think of it as a delicious part of your balanced diet rather than a slip-up on your path to health.

In the end, enjoying food without guilt is all about perspective. It's about recognizing that you're on a journey, and sometimes that journey includes a detour to the land of nachos and chocolate. Give yourself permission to indulge, laugh at the absurdity of life, and remember that food is meant to be enjoyed. By shifting your mindset from guilt to gratitude for the flavors and experiences that food brings, you can finally move forward towards a healthier, happier relationship with what's on your plate. So go ahead, embrace that slice of cake—just maybe don't doomscroll while you're at it!

Chapter 14: Exercise for Everyone: Yes, Even You!

Finding Fun in Movement

Finding fun in movement is like discovering a hidden treasure chest in your backyard. You might think that exercise is just a fancy term for torturing yourself with squats and salads, but let's be real: movement can be a blast! Whether you're a teenager glued to your phone, a busy working adult juggling meetings, or a senior trying to remember where you left your glasses, there's a world of enjoyable ways to get moving. The secret? Turn it into a game! Who says you can't take a dance break while waiting for your microwave popcorn to finish? Throw in some wild moves, and suddenly you're not just heating snacks; you're preparing for your future as the next TikTok star!

Now, let's talk about how to beat the doomscrolling blues. When you find yourself mindlessly swiping through endless feeds of cat memes and conspiracy theories, it's time to take movement into your own hands—literally. Instead of scrolling for hours, why not challenge your friends to a silly walking competition? Bonus points if you do it in a ridiculous costume! Movement doesn't have to be a chore; it can be a spontaneous adventure. So, the next time you find yourself trapped in an echo chamber of negativity, get up, shake it off, and strut your stuff around the block like you're on a runway.

Eating junk food while plopping down on the couch is the classic recipe for inertia. But what if you could spice up your snack time with a little movement? Picture this: every time you grab a handful of chips, you have to do a goofy dance or take a lap around your living room. Not only will you burn some calories, but you might also discover that you've got some seriously impressive dance moves hiding under that couch potato exterior. Plus, when you're up and grooving, those chips might not look as tempting, and you may find yourself reaching for an apple instead. Who knew fruits could be the new snack trend?

For those of you feeling overwhelmed and disorganized, it's time to embrace the magic of movement to clear the clutter—both in your home and your mind. Instead of staring at that pile of laundry like it's a mountain you need to summit, throw on some upbeat music and turn folding into a dance party. You'll not only tackle your chores but also boost your mood and maybe even discover a newfound love for organizing. Just imagine the satisfaction of a tidy space combined with the endorphin rush of a mini workout. It's like hitting two birds with one chore!

Finally, let's address the elephant in the room: sleep deprivation and stress. When life feels like a never-ending to-do list, it's easy to forget about the importance of restorative practices. But here's a fun twist—try incorporating movement into your wind-down routine. Instead of scrolling through your phone and getting lost in the abyss of social media, grab a yoga mat and find a calming video. You'll be amazed at how a little stretching can help clear your mind and lead you to a peaceful night's sleep. Plus, it's a great way to show off your flexibility (or lack thereof) to anyone who dares to peek in. So, let's make movement not just a task, but a joyful part of your everyday life!

Creating an Exercise Routine That Fits Your Life

Creating an exercise routine that fits your life is like trying to fit a square peg in a round hole, especially when your schedule looks like a game of Tetris gone wrong. You wake up, stumble through the day, and somehow end up on the couch, scrolling through social media, wondering how you went from aspiring athlete to a professional snack critic. The first step in crafting an exercise routine is acknowledging your unique lifestyle. Are you a busy bee juggling work and social life? Perhaps you're a Netflix aficionado who has mastered the art of binge-watching without breaking a sweat. Whatever your situation, your routine should embrace who you are, not who you think you should be.

Let's face it: the idea of a gym membership can feel as daunting as a high school chemistry exam. Instead of forcing yourself into a sweaty, crowded space filled with weights that look suspiciously like medieval torture devices, consider activities that bring you joy. Dancing around your living room like no one is watching (because they probably aren't) or going for a brisk walk while pretending you're in a music video are both excellent ways to get your heart pumping. The key is to find movement that feels less like a chore and more like a spontaneous adventure. Remember, if you can't find joy in the journey, you might as well take a nap.

Next up is the myth of the "perfect time" to work out. Spoiler alert: it doesn't exist! Whether you're a morning person who rises with the sun or a night owl who thrives after dark, the best time to exercise is whenever you can squeeze it in. Just think about it: if you wait for the stars to align perfectly, you'll likely just end up scrolling through cat videos instead. So, set a timer, grab that pair of sneakers that are gathering dust under your bed, and treat your workout like a meeting you can't miss. Get creative with your scheduling, and don't be afraid to break up your exercise into bite-sized chunks that fit seamlessly into your day.

Now, let's tackle the concept of accountability because, let's be real, self-discipline is often about as reliable as your friend who always "forgets" their wallet. Find a workout buddy or an enthusiastic pet who can join you on your fitness journey. Share your goals on social media, but only if you promise not to post every single sweaty selfie. The point is to surround yourself with positivity and support—like a motivational cheerleader, but without the pom-poms. This way, you can keep each other on track, swap tips, and maybe even share a few healthy recipes (or at least the ones that don't involve kale).

Finally, remember that consistency is key, but it doesn't mean you should turn into a robot. Life is unpredictable, and sometimes you'll need to adjust your routine like a DJ mixing tracks. Don't beat yourself up if you miss a workout or indulge in a slice of pizza; just get back on track without letting it spiral into a month-long hibernation. Celebrate small victories, like choosing to walk instead of drive, or actually getting through that workout video without muttering expletives. Creating an exercise routine that fits your life is less about being perfect and more about moving forward, one goofy dance move at a time. So, lace up those sneakers, embrace the chaos, and let's get moving!

The Importance of Rest Days

Rest days are like that friend who always tries to convince you to take a break from your marathon gaming sessions. They might seem like a waste of time when you're deep in the grind, but trust me, they're your secret weapon for achieving your goals. Whether you're a teenager cramming for finals, a young adult juggling multiple jobs, or a senior trying to remember where you put your glasses, rest days are essential. It's like giving your brain and body a vacation, and who doesn't love a vacation? You can kick back, binge-watch that new series, or even take a nap that lasts longer than your last workout.

When we think about productivity, we often picture ourselves on a relentless quest for success, battling through every task like a knight slaying dragons. But here's the plot twist: you're not a heroic knight; you're a human being. And humans need rest, or else they turn into grumpy goblins. By taking rest days, you allow your mind to recharge, which can lead to more creativity and better problem-solving skills. So, instead of doomscrolling through social media for hours, which is basically like eating junk food for your brain, consider using that time for some well-deserved R&R. Your future self will thank you.

Let's talk about the science behind rest days. When you're constantly on the move, your cortisol levels skyrocket, and before you know it, you've turned into a stress ball that's about to pop. Rest days help lower those cortisol levels and increase serotonin, which is basically the happiness chemical. You might even find that when you take a break, you're less likely to fall into an echo chamber of negativity. Instead of scrolling through posts that make you question your life choices, you could be out enjoying the sunshine, connecting with friends, or just chilling with a snack that isn't a bag of chips.

Oh, and let's not forget about the glorious power of sleep. Many of us are running on caffeine and sheer willpower, which is like trying to drive a car on empty. Rest days give you the opportunity to catch up on sleep, which is crucial for everything from mood regulation to memory retention. Remember that time you forgot where you put your phone while it was in your hand? Yeah, that's what sleep deprivation does to you. Prioritizing rest can turn those "Where did I leave my keys?" moments into "I'm a fully functional adult" moments.

In a world that glorifies hustle culture, taking rest days can feel like a revolutionary act. It's time to break free from the inertia loop of constant busyness and embrace the idea that doing nothing is sometimes the most productive thing you can do. So, whether you're decluttering your space, binge-watching a show, or just staring at the ceiling, remember that these moments of rest are crucial for your mental and physical health. Embrace them, laugh at the chaos of life, and move forward with renewed energy and zest.

Chapter 15: Building Positive Habits

The Science of Habit Formation

Habit formation is like training a puppy: it takes patience, consistency, and maybe a few treats along the way. Whether you're a teenager scrolling through social media instead of doing homework or an adult buried under a mountain of tasks and junk food wrappers, understanding how habits work can be a game changer. Our brains are wired to seek pleasure and avoid pain, which is why that couch feels so inviting and the fridge calls your name at midnight. But don't worry, you're not alone in this struggle. Everyone from busy professionals to seniors trying to remember where they left their glasses can relate to the struggle of forming better habits.

The science behind habit formation begins with something called the habit loop, a three-part process that includes a cue, a routine, and a reward. Imagine the cue is your phone buzzing with notifications, prompting you to doomscroll for hours. The routine? That's you mindlessly scrolling through memes. And the reward? Well, it's that temporary dopamine high that makes you feel good until you realize you've just spent the last hour watching videos of cats failing at jumping. Understanding this loop can help you recognize when you're stuck in an inertia loop and pave the way to break free from it.

Now, let's talk about breaking bad habits. You know that moment when you open the fridge and find not a single vegetable in sight? That's a cue for a junk food binge. Instead, try swapping out the snacks for something healthier. It's not just about willpower; it's about making it easier to choose the better option. Set your environment up for success! If you want to avoid junk food, stock your pantry with fruits, nuts, and maybe a few dark chocolate bars for those moments when you really need a treat. Remember, if you put kale in the fridge, it's not going to magically turn into a pizza.

Creating a daily routine is like giving your day a GPS. It helps you navigate through tasks without veering off into the chaos of clutter and procrastination. Start small—maybe dedicate ten minutes each morning to plan your day. You'll feel like a productivity ninja! And speaking of ninjas, let's not forget sleep. Adequate rest is crucial for habit formation; without it, you'll be more forgetful than a goldfish. Set a bedtime that allows for at least seven hours of sleep, and watch how it transforms your ability to tackle that to-do list, no ninja skills required.

Lastly, let's sprinkle in some humor: if you're feeling overwhelmed, just remember that even the most organized person has a junk drawer. The key is not to aim for perfection but to focus on progress. Celebrate small wins, whether it's finally organizing that closet or managing to cook a vegetable without burning it. Each step forward is a victory on the path to forming healthier habits. So grab a snack, put on your favorite show, and get ready to move forward—just make sure it's not a show about procrastinating!

Stacking Habits: A Two-for-One Deal

Stacking habits is like getting two scoops of ice cream for the price of one, but instead of chocolate and vanilla, you get productivity and positivity. Imagine this: you're scrolling through your phone, and suddenly you realize you've spent hours lost in an endless loop of cat videos and conspiracy theories about pigeons being government drones. Instead of doomscrolling, why not stack a positive habit onto it? While you're waiting for the latest conspiracy to unravel, you can do a quick set of squats or practice mindfulness for a minute. Your brain gets the dopamine hit from the phone, but your body gets a workout too. It's like tricking your brain into thinking it's having fun while you sneak in some health benefits.

Now, let's talk about food. If you're anything like me, the siren call of junk food can be hard to resist, especially when the fridge is calling your name louder than a toddler in a toy store. But why not turn that midnight snack into a habit-stacking opportunity? Next time you reach for that family-sized bag of chips, grab a handful of nuts or some fruit first. It's a two-for-one deal: you satisfy that late-night craving while giving your body a little love. Plus, nuts are a great source of healthy fats, and fruit is packed with vitamins—think of them as the superheroes of the snack world, ready to save you from yourself.

Let's not forget about the clutter that seems to multiply faster than rabbits. You walk into your room and think, "Did I invite a tornado in here?" Instead of feeling overwhelmed by the mess, you can stack a cleaning habit with something you love. Blast your favorite tunes and tidy up while you dance like nobody's watching. You'll be amazed at how much you can accomplish when you turn a chore into a mini-party. By the end of it, you'll have a cleaner space and a great workout—talk about a win-win situation!

For those feeling lost in the chaos of life, habit stacking can be your GPS out of the inertia loop. If you struggle with procrastination, pair a task you despise with something you enjoy. For example, if you have to sit down to study but would rather watch paint dry, stack it with your favorite podcast. You get to learn something new while tackling that to-do list. Before you know it, studying becomes less of a chore and more of a fun, enlightening experience. Who knew adulting could be so entertaining?

Lastly, let's address the sleep-deprived zombies wandering around like extras from a horror movie. If you're battling insomnia and can't seem to put down the screens, stack your bedtime routine with calming activities. Try reading a book or practicing some gentle stretches before bed instead of scrolling through social media. You'll be getting your dose of relaxation while also creating a separation from the digital chaos. With each stacked habit, you're not just moving forward; you're gliding along like a pro on a slip-n-slide of success. So go ahead, start stacking those habits and enjoy the ride!

Tracking Progress: It's All About the Journey

Tracking progress is like trying to find your way through a foggy maze while holding a map upside down. You might feel lost at times, but each twist and turn is part of the adventure. As teenagers, young adults, busy workers, and even seniors grapple with the chaos of daily life, it's crucial to remember that your journey is not just about reaching a destination. It's about the hilarious missteps and epic fails along the way. So grab that metaphorical map, and let's navigate through the quagmire of doomscrolling, junk food, and the relentless echo chambers of the internet together.

First, let's address the elephant in the room: doomscrolling. It's like binge-watching a terrible series that you know will leave you feeling empty inside. You get sucked into an endless feed of negativity, and before you know it, you've lost three hours of your life. Tracking your progress means recognizing when you've spent too much time in the digital rabbit hole. Set a timer, put down the phone, and ask yourself, "Is this what I want my life to look like?" Spoiler alert: the answer is usually no. Your time is precious, so reclaim it before it disappears like your willpower in front of a pizza.

Now let's talk about food because let's face it, who doesn't love a good snack? The Standard American Diet is a bit like that friend who always convinces you to go for fast food instead of hitting the gym. Sure, it's quick and easy, but it's also a recipe for feeling sluggish and cranky. Tracking your progress in eating habits doesn't mean you have to turn into a kale-eating robot. Instead, start by swapping out one junk food item for something healthier each week. You'll be surprised at how quickly those small changes add up. And if you slip up and demolish a bag of chips? Just laugh it off and keep moving forward.

Life can feel like a never-ending to-do list where everything is important, yet nothing gets done. Trust me, I've been there, standing in front of a pile of laundry that has become a mountain of despair. The key to tracking progress in this area is to create a daily routine that doesn't make you want to curl up under your blanket. Prioritize tasks, set small achievable goals, and celebrate victories, no matter how tiny they may seem. Did you manage to get off the couch and fold that laundry? High five! Did you write a single sentence of that essay? You're basically Shakespeare now. Progress is progress, even if it's measured in baby steps.

Finally, let's not forget about the importance of mental health and emotional resilience. Life is a rollercoaster, and sometimes it feels like we're just hanging on for dear life. Being overwhelmed is a common theme, especially for those of us juggling work, school, and the occasional existential crisis. Tracking your progress in this area means acknowledging your feelings and finding healthy outlets for stress. Whether it's through exercise, meditation, or just a good laugh with friends, prioritize what makes you feel good. Remember, it's perfectly okay to seek help when you need it. You don't have to face life's challenges alone, and asking for support is a sign of strength, not weakness.

So, as you embark on this journey of tracking progress, remember to embrace the messy, chaotic, and sometimes ridiculous nature of life. Each day is an opportunity to make better choices, laugh at your mistakes, and learn how to navigate through the clutter. Your journey may not always look pretty, but it's uniquely yours, and that's what makes it beautiful. Keep moving forward, one hilarious misadventure at a time!

Chapter 16: Mindful Technology Use

Digital Detox: The Ultimate Challenge

In a world where our smartphones are practically glued to our hands, the idea of a digital detox might sound as appealing as asking a cat to take a bath. Between the endless scroll of memes, TikTok dances, and news that could make even the cheeriest person question their life choices, it's no wonder we're all feeling a tad overwhelmed. So, what if we took a break from our screens and gave our brains a much-needed vacation? Sure, it might feel like going cold turkey on chocolate during a week-long diet, but the rewards could be sweeter than a double chocolate fudge cake.

Imagine this: instead of doomscrolling through the latest headlines that make you want to pull your hair out, you could dive into a book or even try that hobby you've been saying you'll pick up "any day now." You know, the one that involves more than just your thumbs swiping up and down. Being plugged in 24/7 can make you feel like you're on a hamster wheel, running fast but getting absolutely nowhere. It's time to hit the pause button on those social media algorithms that know you better than your own family and take a step back to figure out what you really want out of life—besides just another episode of your favorite show.

Now, let's talk about echo chambers. You know, those cozy little corners of the internet where everyone thinks the same way you do, and any opposing opinion is met with the digital equivalent of throwing tomatoes? It's easy to fall into this trap, especially when you're already feeling overwhelmed or anxious about the world. A digital detox can help break those chains of negativity and open your mind to new perspectives. Plus, you might find out that there are other people out there who enjoy pineapple on pizza, and maybe—just maybe—you won't have to block your cousin over their questionable food choices.

Of course, setting aside your devices won't magically fix all your problems. If you've been relying on junk food as a comfort during your late-night scrolling sessions, you might need to reconsider your snack choices. A detox isn't just about unplugging; it's about filling that newfound free time with healthier habits—like cooking, exercising, or even just staring out the window contemplating life's big questions, like why we never have enough matching socks. When you replace mindless munching with mindfulness, you'll find yourself feeling more energized and ready to tackle those neglected goals that seem to be gathering dust on your to-do list.

Ultimately, a digital detox is like hitting the refresh button on your life. It's not about deprivation; it's about making room for growth, creativity, and that sweet, sweet clarity. You may rediscover the joy of writing down your thoughts instead of typing them or taking a walk without documenting every step on social media. So, embrace the challenge! You might just find that life outside the digital bubble is more vibrant, fulfilling, and a lot less stressful. After all, the real world has a lot more to offer than endless notifications and a sea of clutter. Now, go ahead and unplug— you've got a life to live!

Setting Boundaries with Your Devices

Setting boundaries with your devices is like trying to train a puppy. At first, they're adorable, but soon you realize they're chewing on your favorite shoes and ignoring your commands. Your phone is that pesky puppy, demanding attention at all hours, and if you don't set some ground rules, it's going to take over your life. You might find yourself scrolling through social media at 2 a.m., convinced that you need to know what your third cousin's neighbor had for breakfast. Newsflash: you don't. Establishing boundaries is like putting your phone in a time-out; it's necessary for your sanity.

Start by designating specific times for device use. Think of it as your personal tech curfew. Set aside certain hours for checking emails, scrolling through social media, or binge-watching that show you promised yourself you'd only watch one episode of. Trust me, those "just one more episode" promises are as reliable as a chocolate teapot. By creating a schedule, you'll be less likely to fall into the doomscrolling abyss, where time disappears faster than snacks at a party. Plus, you'll reclaim those precious hours for more productive activities, like actually talking to your friends in person. Remember them?

Next, consider the content you consume. Algorithms can be as sneaky as a cat burglar, luring you into echo chambers that feed your negativity. You've got to take the wheel and navigate your online experience. Follow accounts that inspire you, make you laugh, or even teach you something new. If your feed is filled with negativity, it's like bingeing on junk food; it feels good in the moment but leaves you feeling sluggish and regretful afterward. Curate your digital space as if it were a garden; pull out the weeds and let the flowers bloom.

Now, let's tackle the clutter. No, not just the piles of laundry sitting in the corner of your room, but the mental clutter that comes from constant notifications and alerts. Turn off non-essential notifications, and watch your stress levels drop faster than a lead balloon. You don't need your phone buzzing every time someone comments on a post, especially when it interrupts your Netflix marathon. Treat your phone like a friend who talks too much:

sometimes, you need to put them on mute to enjoy some peace and quiet.

Finally, remember that your devices should serve you, not the other way around. Use apps that promote mindfulness instead of mindlessness. Set reminders to take breaks, stretch, or even go for a walk. Think of these boundaries as a gentle nudge towards a healthier relationship with technology. You want to move forward in life, not be stuck in a loop of procrastination and distraction. So, reclaim your time, set those boundaries, and watch as you transform from a device-dependent zombie into a goal-crushing superstar.

Cultivating Mindfulness in a Hyper-Connected World

In a world where our phones are practically attached to our hands, cultivating mindfulness might feel like trying to find a needle in a haystack—or rather, a moment of silence in a cacophony of notifications. Picture this: you're scrolling through your social media feed, and before you know it, hours have vanished as you dive deep into the rabbit hole of memes, cat videos, and heated debates over pineapple on pizza. Instead of letting algorithms dictate your mood (hint: they rarely choose happiness), it's time to take a step back, put down the phone, and embrace the art of being present. Mindfulness is not just a trendy buzzword; it's your ticket to a more fulfilling life amidst the chaos, and it might just save you from the doomscrolling abyss.

Now, let's talk about junk food. We all know that moment when you're standing in front of the fridge at midnight, contemplating whether to devour that leftover pizza or go for an apple. Spoiler alert: pizza is usually the winner. But what if, instead of succumbing to late-night cravings, you practiced mindfulness? Imagine savoring that slice of pizza—really tasting each gooey bite while also appreciating how your body feels afterward. By cultivating awareness around your eating habits, you can swap out the junk for more nourishing options without feeling deprived. It's about balance, not a total ban on your favorite foods. After all, life is too short to live without the occasional pizza party.

As we navigate through our increasingly busy lives, time management can feel like trying to juggle flaming swords—exciting but slightly hazardous. When you're overwhelmed with tasks, it's easy to fall into the inertia loop, where everything feels too much, and nothing gets done. Instead of letting that pile of laundry mock you from the corner, try breaking your tasks into bite-sized pieces. Set a timer for 10 minutes and tackle that mountain of clutter. You'll be amazed at how quickly you can turn chaos into order when you approach it mindfully. Plus, you might discover a long-lost sock or two along the way.

Speaking of socks, let's not forget about our mental health and emotional resilience. In this hyper-connected world, anxiety can feel like your unwanted roommate who refuses to leave. When stress levels rise, it's tempting to binge-watch another season of that show you swore you'd finish "tomorrow." Instead, practice mindfulness by incorporating short meditation or deep-breathing exercises into your day. Even a few minutes of focused breathing can help you reclaim your mental space and reduce that overwhelming feeling. With practice, you'll find that you can tackle challenges with a clearer mind, and maybe even find the motivation to get off the couch and go for a walk—socks and all.

Finally, let's wrap up with a reminder that growth doesn't have to be a daunting journey filled with stress and disorganization. Embracing minimalism and decluttering your life can free up not only your physical space but also your mental bandwidth. When you let go of what no longer serves you—be it a pile of old magazines or that hoodie you've kept since high school—you create room for new experiences and positive habits. So, grab a trash bag and start tossing! You'll be surprised at how much lighter you feel after decluttering your space and mind. After all, a clear space leads to a clear mind, and who doesn't want that in this whirlwind we call life?

Chapter 17: Moving Forward: Your Roadmap to Growth

Reflecting on Your Journey

As we gather our scattered thoughts and aim to reflect on our journey, let's take a moment to appreciate the chaos that often feels like our constant companion. Picture it: a swirling tornado of social media notifications, junk food wrappers, and to-do lists that seem to multiply like rabbits. If you've ever felt like you're stuck in an inertia loop where the only thing moving is your Netflix queue, you're not alone! Embracing the messiness of life is the first step toward making sense of it all. Remember, even the best journeys start with a few wrong turns and a detour through the drive-thru.

Now, let's talk about doomscrolling. It's like a digital black hole where productivity goes to die. You start with the best intentions, perhaps checking the news for a quick five minutes, and before you know it, you've spiraled down a rabbit hole of cat memes and conspiracy theories. It's a slippery slope to a screen-induced stupor, where you end up questioning if your life choices really matter or if you should just buy a one-way ticket to the Land of the Lost Hobbies. The key here is to recognize when scrolling turns into a full-blown binge and take a break. Seriously, your brain will thank you for it—just think of all the books you could read or the hobbies you could revive!

As we navigate through this whirlwind, let's address the elephant in the room: the standard American diet. If you're living on a diet of pizza rolls and energy drinks, it's time for a change. Sure, junk food is delicious and convenient, but it won't fuel your journey to becoming the best version of yourself. Picture your body as a car—would you fill it with low-octane petrol and expect it to zoom past the competition? Nah, you'd want premium fuel! So, swap out those snacks for something that won't leave you feeling like a sluggish potato. Your brain needs nutrients to function and to fend off the overwhelming stress that life throws your way.

Speaking of stress, let's not forget the importance of building positive habits and daily routines. If your idea of a daily routine involves hitting snooze until your alarm clock gives up on life, it's time to reassess. Crafting a routine doesn't have to feel like a chore; think of it as creating a personalized playlist for your day. Start small! Maybe it's just drinking a glass of water in the morning instead of reaching for your phone. Gradually, these tiny tweaks can snowball into something magnificent. You'll go from feeling like a disorganized jigsaw puzzle to a masterpiece that even Picasso would admire—minus the confusion and existential dread.

Lastly, let's tackle the clutter—both in your physical space and your mental landscape. If your workspace looks like a tornado just hit it, or if your bedroom resembles a scene from a hoarding reality show, it's time to declutter. Embrace minimalism! It's not just for Instagram influencers; it's for anyone who feels overwhelmed by the sheer amount of stuff we accumulate. Start with one small area, maybe a drawer or a corner of your desk, and tackle it like it's an epic quest. As you clear away the chaos, you'll find that your mind can breathe a little easier, making room for creativity, productivity, and the occasional dance party in your living room. So grab that trash bag, take a deep breath, and let's start reflecting on this wild journey with a sense of humor and a whole lot of heart!

Creating a Personalized Action Plan

Creating a personalized action plan is like crafting your own superhero costume—it's all about finding what fits you best while also making you feel invincible. First things first, grab a pen and paper or your favorite note-taking app. Begin by jotting down your biggest frustrations and distractions. Are you spending more time scrolling through cat videos than actually achieving your goals? Do you get lost in the endless abyss of social media algorithms that seem to know you better than your best friend? Embrace the chaos of your life, and let's transform that mess into a manageable plan that even your most chaotic days can't derail.

Next, let's talk about your goals. Yes, those pesky little things that seem to elude you like your socks in the dryer. Break them down into bite-sized, achievable pieces—think of them as snacks rather than an entire buffet. Maybe you want to eat healthier but can't resist that late-night pizza run. Instead of vowing to become a kale-eating machine overnight, start by swapping one snack a day for something green. Remember, Rome wasn't built in a day, and neither is your ideal life. Take small, consistent steps to build momentum without feeling overwhelmed. You don't want to fall into the inertia loop where doing nothing feels easier than doing something.

Now, let's tackle the clutter—both physical and mental. Your room might look like a tornado hit it, and your brain feels like a crowded subway during rush hour. Start decluttering by picking one area at a time. Maybe it's your desk, your closet, or even your mind. Set a timer for 10 minutes and go wild! You'll be surprised at how much you can accomplish when you're racing against the clock. And don't forget to clear your digital clutter too. Unsubscribe from the emails that make you feel like you're drowning in a sea of sales pitches. Your inbox can be a peaceful oasis instead of a chaotic jungle.

As you begin to see progress, it's time to incorporate some daily routines into your life. Routines are like the training wheels for adulthood; they keep you from falling flat on your face while navigating through the chaos. Try setting a specific time to wake up, eat, and wind down. Even if you're not a morning person, setting a routine can make your day feel less like a free-for-all. Adding just a few minutes of exercise, even if it's just a brisk walk, can do wonders for your mood and energy levels. Plus, it's a great excuse to avoid that couch potato lifestyle.

Finally, celebrate your victories—no matter how small they may seem. Did you manage to resist the urge to scroll through your phone before bed? Give yourself a mental high-five! Recognizing your achievements keeps you motivated and helps build resilience against setbacks. Remember, everyone has their struggles, and it's okay to feel overwhelmed sometimes. But with a personalized action plan in place, you're not just surviving; you're thriving. So, throw on that superhero cape and get ready to conquer your goals, one quirky step at a time.

Embracing Change: The Adventure Awaits!

Embracing change is like jumping into a swimming pool on a hot summer day: it's terrifying at first, but once you're in, you wonder why you hesitated. For teenagers and young adults, change often feels more like a last-minute group project where everyone has forgotten to do their part. The key is to shift your perspective and start seeing change not as an enemy but as a quirky friend who shows up uninvited with a bag of snacks. Sure, it might take some time to adjust to the unpredictability of life, but that's where the adventure truly lies. So, let's dive in and discover why embracing change can be the best decision you ever make (next to finally throwing away that half-eaten bag of chips in your room).

For those of us who have fallen into the doomscrolling abyss, where time disappears faster than your willpower at a buffet, it's time to break free. Imagine your phone as a mischievous gremlin, luring you into echo chambers and feeding you junk food for the mind. With every swipe, you're trapped in a cycle of negativity and distraction. Instead, replace that screen time with a new hobby or a quick workout—something that makes your brain tingle with excitement instead of dread. Trust me, your future self will thank you when you're not staring blankly at the ceiling at 3 a.m., wondering why your life feels like a poorly scripted sitcom.

Now, let's tackle the clutter. You know, that mountain of clothes in the corner that's grown a personality? It's time to channel your inner minimalist and start decluttering your space and mind. Think of your room as a blank canvas, and you're the artist with a messy palette. Start small—tackle one drawer at a time, and don't be afraid to throw out anything that doesn't spark joy, like that shirt you haven't worn since the '90s. By creating a clean space, you'll find it easier to focus on the things that truly matter, like your goals and dreams, rather than dodging the Lego pieces scattered across your floor.

Feeling overwhelmed is as common as forgetting where you put your keys. With busy lives, it's easy to lose sight of our priorities. But here's the twist: you don't have to do everything at once. Break your tasks into bite-sized pieces. If you have a big project looming, think of it as a pizza—slice it up into manageable portions. And if pizza is involved, who wouldn't want to tackle that? Plus, by setting mini-goals, you'll feel that sweet rush of accomplishment, which is way better than binge-watching another season of a show you don't even like.

Lastly, let's talk about the importance of sleep. You might think you can survive on caffeine and good intentions, but your body disagrees. Treat sleep like the precious treasure it is. Create a bedtime routine that doesn't involve scrolling through your phone until you fall into a digital coma. Instead, wind down with a book, some light stretching, or even meditation. Remember, a rested mind is a powerful one, ready to take on the adventures that change brings. So go ahead, embrace that change, laugh at the chaos, and watch how your life transforms into an exciting journey filled with growth, laughter, and maybe even a little less clutter!

Notes:

www.ingramcontent.com/pod-product-compliance
Lightning Source LLC
Chambersburg PA
CBHW060336050426
42449CB00011B/2767